Hands-On Exploratory Data Analysis with R

Become an expert in exploratory data analysis using
R packages

Radhika Datar
Harish Garg

BIRMINGHAM - MUMBAI

Hands-On Exploratory Data Analysis with R

Commissioning Editor: Pravin Dhandre
Acquisition Editor: Nelson Morris
Content Development Editor: Pratik Andrade
Technical Editor: Nilesh Sawakhande
Copy Editor: Safis Editing
Language Support Editors: Storm Mann, Sophie Rogers
Project Coordinator: Namrata Swetta
Proofreader: Safis Editing
Indexer: Priyanka Dhadke
Graphics: Jisha Chirayil
Production Coordinator: Jyoti Chauhan

First published: May 2019

Production reference: 1310519

Published by Packt Publishing Ltd.
Livery Place
35 Livery Street
Birmingham
B3 2PB, UK.

ISBN 978-1-78980-437-9

www.packtpub.com

I would like to dedicate this book to my parents, and my in-laws, for their sacrifices, valuable support, and for exemplifying the power of determination.

Also, to my husband, Omkar, for being a loving and supportive partner all throughout our journey.

– Radhika Datar

`mapt.io`

Mapt is an online digital library that gives you full access to over 5,000 books and videos, as well as industry leading tools to help you plan your personal development and advance your career. For more information, please visit our website.

Why subscribe?

- Spend less time learning and more time coding with practical eBooks and Videos from over 4,000 industry professionals

- Improve your learning with Skill Plans built especially for you

- Get a free eBook or video every month

- Mapt is fully searchable

- Copy and paste, print, and bookmark content

Packt.com

Did you know that Packt offers eBook versions of every book published, with PDF and ePub files available? You can upgrade to the eBook version at `www.packt.com` and as a print book customer, you are entitled to a discount on the eBook copy. Get in touch with us at `customercare@packtpub.com` for more details.

At `www.packt.com`, you can also read a collection of free technical articles, sign up for a range of free newsletters, and receive exclusive discounts and offers on Packt books and eBooks.

Contributors

About the authors

Radhika Datar has more than 5 years' experience in software development and content writing. She is well versed in frameworks such as Python, PHP, and Java, and regularly provides training on them. She has been working with Educba and Eduonix as a training consultant since June 2016, while also working as a freelance academic writer in data science and data analytics. She obtained her master's degree from the Symbiosis Institute of Computer Studies and Research and her bachelor's degree from K. J. Somaiya College of Science and Commerce.

Harish Garg is a Principal Software Developer, author, and co-founder of a software development and training company, Bignumworks. Harish has more than 19 years of experience in a wide variety of technologies, including blockchain, data science and enterprise software. During this time, he has worked for companies such as McAfee, Intel, etc.

About the reviewer

Prashant Sahu has a B.Tech. from NIT Rourkela (2003), and is currently pursuing his PhD at the Indian Institute of Technology, Bombay (2014 onward) in the area of instrumentation, data analytics, modeling, and simulation applied to semi-conductor materials and devices. He is currently employed as the head of training services with Tech Smart Systems, Pune. He has more than 15 years' experience and has handled many projects in the sphere of academia and industry. He has also delivered several training courses for academia, as well as corporate training courses for software companies across India in data analytics and data science using Python and R. He is also an external examiner for B.E./M.E. projects, and a member of the Syllabus Revision Committee at the University of Pune (Computer and IT).

Packt is searching for authors like you

If you're interested in becoming an author for Packt, please visit `authors.packtpub.com` and apply today. We have worked with thousands of developers and tech professionals, just like you, to help them share their insight with the global tech community. You can make a general application, apply for a specific hot topic that we are recruiting an author for, or submit your own idea.

Table of Contents

Section 2: Univariate, Time Series, and Multivariate Data

Preface

As the name suggests, Hands-On Exploratory Data Analysis with R practically demonstrates the complete process of exploratory data analysis. In this book you will learn about the complete process of exploratory data analysis using R and some of its most popular and powerful packages. You will understand the concepts of data analysis right from data ingestion, data cleaning, and data manipulation, to applying statistical techniques and visualizing hidden patterns. By the end of this book, you will be able to expand your real-world R knowledge by means of practical real-world data analysis projects.

Who this book is for

This book is for you if you are looking to build a strong foundation in data analysis. Whether you are a data analyst, data engineer, software engineer, product manager, or anybody who is involved with data in any way, this book will sharpen your skills in the overarching workflow of exploratory data analysis.

What this book covers

Chapter 1, *Setting Up Our Data Analysis Environment*, introduces the overall goal of this book. This chapter stipulates how exploratory data analysis benefits business and has a significant impact across almost all verticals.

Chapter 2, *Importing Diverse Datasets*, demonstrates practical, hands-on code examples on reading in all kinds of data into R for exploratory data analysis. This chapter also covers how to use advanced options while importing datasets such as delimited data, Excel data, JSON data, and data from web APIs.

Chapter 3, *Examining, Cleaning, and Filtering*, introduces how to identify and clean missing and erroneous data formats. This chapter also covers concepts such as data manipulation, wrangling, and reshaping.

Chapter 4, *Visualizing Data Graphically with ggplot2*, demonstrates how to draw different kinds of plots and charts, including scatter plots, histograms, probability plots, residual plots, boxplots, and block plots.

Chapter 5, *Creating Aesthetically Pleasing Reports with knitr and R Markdown*, explains how to use RStudio to wrap your code, graphics, plots, and findings in a complete and informative data analysis report. The chapter will also look at how to publish these in different formats for different audiences using R Markdown and packages such as knitr.

Chapter 6, *Univariate and Control Datasets*, takes a real-world univariate and control dataset and runs an entire exploratory data analysis workflow on it using the R packages and techniques.

Chapter 7, *Time Series Datasets*, introduces a time series dataset and describes how to use exploratory data analysis techniques to analyze this data.

Chapter 8, *Multivariate Datasets*, introduces a dataset from the multivariate problem category. This chapter explains how to use exploratory data analysis techniques to analyze this data, as well as how to use the exploratory data analysis techniques of the star plot, the scatter plot matrix, the conditioning plot, and their principal components.

Chapter 9, *Multi-Factor Datasets*, introduces a multi-factor dataset and explains how to use exploratory data analysis techniques to analyze this data.

Chapter 10, *Handling Optimization and Regression Data Problems*, introduces a dataset from the regression problem category and describes how to use exploratory data analysis techniques to analyze this data. It also shows how to learn and apply these exploratory data analysis techniques.

Chapter 11, *Next Steps*, covers how to build a roadmap for yourself to consolidate the skills you have learned in this book and gain further expertise in the field of data science with R.

To get the most out of this book

In order to get the most out of this book, you should already be familiar with the basics of the R programming language and you should possess at least a rudimentary knowledge of data analysis, irrespective of the tool or programming language. If you would like to learn the basics of R, we recommend one of our excellent Packt titles.

Download the example code files

You can download the example code files for this book from your account at www.packt.com. If you purchased this book elsewhere, you can visit www.packt.com/support and register to have the files emailed directly to you.

You can download the code files by following these steps:

1. Log in or register at `www.packt.com`.
2. Select the **SUPPORT** tab.
3. Click on **Code Downloads & Errata**.
4. Enter the name of the book in the **Search** box and follow the onscreen instructions.

Once the file is downloaded, please make sure that you unzip or extract the folder using the latest version of:

- WinRAR/7-Zip for Windows
- Zipeg/iZip/UnRarX for Mac
- 7-Zip/PeaZip for Linux

The code bundle for the book is also hosted on GitHub at **`https://github.com/PacktPublishing/Hands-On-Exploratory-Data-Analysis-with-R`**. In case there's an update to the code, it will be updated on the existing GitHub repository.

We also have other code bundles from our rich catalog of books and videos available at `https://github.com/PacktPublishing/`. Check them out!

Download the color images

We also provide a PDF file that has color images of the screenshots/diagrams used in this book. You can download it here: `http://www.packtpub.com/sites/default/files/downloads/9781789804379_ColorImages.pdf`.

Code in Action

Visit the following link to check out videos of the code being run:
`http://bit.ly/30X4RGO`

Conventions used

There are a number of text conventions used throughout this book.

`CodeInText`: Indicates code words in text, database table names, folder names, filenames, file extensions, pathnames, dummy URLs, user input, and Twitter handles. Here is an example: "Mount the downloaded `WebStorm-10*.dmg` disk image file as another disk in your system."

A block of code is set as follows:

```
html, body, #map {
  height: 100%;
  margin: 0;
  padding: 0
}
```

When we wish to draw your attention to a particular part of a code block, the relevant lines or items are set in bold:

```
[default]
exten => s,1,Dial(Zap/1|30)
exten => s,2,Voicemail(u100)
exten => s,102,Voicemail(b100)
exten => i,1,Voicemail(s0)
```

Any command-line input or output is written as follows:

```
$ mkdir css
$ cd css
```

Bold: Indicates a new term, an important word, or words that you see on screen. For example, words in menus or dialog boxes appear in the text like this. Here is an example: "Select **System info** from the **Administration** panel."

 Warnings or important notes appear like this.

 Tips and tricks appear like this.

Get in touch

Feedback from our readers is always welcome.

General feedback: If you have questions about any aspect of this book, mention the book title in the subject of your message and email us at customercare@packtpub.com.

Errata: Although we have taken every care to ensure the accuracy of our content, mistakes do happen. If you have found a mistake in this book, we would be grateful if you would report this to us. Please visit www.packt.com/submit-errata, selecting your book, clicking on the Errata Submission Form link, and entering the details.

Piracy: If you come across any illegal copies of our works in any form on the internet, we would be grateful if you would provide us with the location address or website name. Please contact us at copyright@packt.com with a link to the material.

If you are interested in becoming an author: If there is a topic that you have expertise in, and you are interested in either writing or contributing to a book, please visit authors.packtpub.com.

Reviews

Please leave a review. Once you have read and used this book, why not leave a review on the site that you purchased it from? Potential readers can then see and use your unbiased opinion to make purchase decisions, we at Packt can understand what you think about our products, and our authors can see your feedback on their book. Thank you!

For more information about Packt, please visit packt.com.

Section 1: Setting Up Data Analysis Environment

We will start by setting up the R toolkit for exploratory data analysis, dig deep into the concepts of importing data into R, cleaning and manipulating data, and then move onto visualizing data, before producing reproducible data reports.

The following chapters will be covered in this section:

- Chapter 1, *Setting Up Our Data Analysis Environment*
- Chapter 2, *Importing Diverse Datasets*
- Chapter 3, *Examining, Cleaning, and Filtering*
- Chapter 4, *Graphically Visualize Data with ggplot2*
- Chapter 5, *Creating Aesthetically Pleasing Reports with Knitr and R Markdown*

Setting Up Our Data Analysis Environment

1

In this chapter, we will look at how **Exploratory Data Analysis** (**EDA**) benefits businesses and has a significant impact on almost all vertical markets.

EDA is nothing but a pattern of analyzing datasets to summarize their main features, mostly with visual methods. We will list the R packages and tools that are required to do EDA. We will also focus on the installation procedure and setting up the packages for the EDA environment from an R perspective.

The following topics will be covered in this chapter:

- The benefits of EDA across vertical markets
- The most popular R packages for EDA
- Installing the required R packages and tools

Technical requirements

R is an open source software that is platform independent. All you need to do is download the particular package from the following links:

The following steps are used to install R in your system:

- You need to have the R language installed. Download the R installer from here: `https://cran.r--project.org/`.
- We recommend using **RStudio**. If you don't already have it installed, you can get it from the following link: `https://www.rstudio.com/products/rstudio/download`.
- Check that R and RStudio are working.
- Install the R packages required for the workshop.

The first time you open the RStudio user interface after installation, it will look as shown in the following screenshot:

- You will also need to have prior knowledge of the R programming language. Packt has a wide range of books and video titles that are available for this purpose.
- The code for this chapter is available at the following link: https://github.com/PacktPublishing/Hands-On-Exploratory-Data-Analysis-with-R.

The benefits of EDA across vertical markets

Every organization today produces and relies on a lot of data in their everyday processes. Before making assumptions and decisions based on this data, organizations need to be able to understand it. EDA enables data analysts and data scientists to bring this information to the right people. It is the most important step on which a data-driven organization should focus its energy and resources.

Having practical tools in hand for carrying out EDA helps data analysts and data scientists produce reproducible and knowledgeable data analysis results. R is one of the most popular data analysis environments, so it makes sense to equip your data analysis teams with powerful R techniques to make the most of their EDA skills.

At the time of writing this book, there are more than 13,000 R packages available according to CRAN. You can get R packages for all kinds of tasks and domains. For our purpose, we will be concentrating on a particular set of R packages that are considered the best by the R community for the purpose of EDA. Some of the packages that we are going to cover may not be directly related to EDA, but they are relevant for other stages of dealing with the data, as indicated by the following diagram:

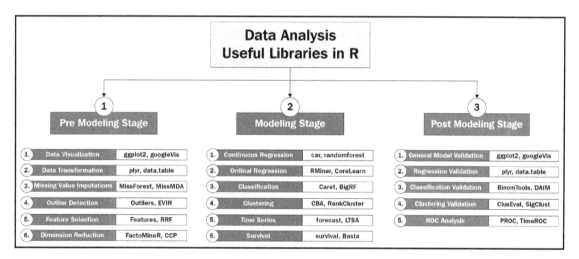

We will introduce these packages briefly in this chapter and go into more detail as the book progresses. The different stages are as mentioned as follows:

- **Pre Modeling Stage**: This stage involves the manipulation of the data frame based on **Data Visualization, Data Transformation, Missing Value Imputations, Outlier Detection, Feature Selection**, and **Dimension Reduction**.
- **Modeling Stage**: This stage is considered as an intermediate stage that involves **Continuous Regression, Ordinal Regression, Classification, Clustering**, and **Time Series** with **Survival**.
- **Post Modeling Stage**: This stage is considered as a final stage where only output interpretation is considered on high priority. It includes the implementation of various algorithms such as clustering, classification, and regression.

Manipulating data

Before you can start exploring your data, you first need to import it into your data analysis environment. There are many types of data, ranging from plain data in comma-separated value files to binary data in databases. Different R packages are equipped to handle these different kinds of data expertly and to import them almost ready for use in our environment. Since we are using R and RStudio, we will describe some of the most powerful R packages to import data in the following sections:

- readr: readr can be used to read flat, *rectangular* data into R. It works with both comma-separated and tab-separated values.
- readxl: We can use the readxl package to read data from MS Excel files.
- jsonlite: Web services have increasingly started to provide data in a JSON format. The jsonlite package is a good way to import this kind of data into R.
- httr, rvest: httr, and rvest are very good packages to get data from the web, either from web APIs or by web scraping.
- DBI: DBI is used to read data from relational databases into R.

Examining, cleaning, and filtering data

The next steps after importing the data are to examine it and check for missing or erroneous data. We then need to clean the data and apply filters and selections. Different kinds of datasets need different approaches to carry out these steps. R has powerful packages to handle this and some of them are as follows:

- dplyr: dplyr is a powerful R package that provides methods to make examining, cleaning, and filtering data fast and easy.
- tidyr: The tidyr package helps to organize messy data for easier data analysis.
- stringr: The stringr package provides methods and techniques of working with string data efficiently.
- forcats: Factors are widely used while doing data analysis in R. The forcats package makes it easy to work with factors.
- lubridate: lubridate makes wrangling date-time data quick and easy.
- hms: hms is a great package for handling datasets that include data with **time of day** values.
- blob: Not all data always comes stored in plain ASCII text; you sometimes have to deal with binary data formats. The blob package makes this easy.

Visualizing data

Visualizing data is one of the best ways to carry out graphical EDA. Visualizing data with plots and charts allows us to discover facts about the data that may not be very obvious when applying quantitative EDA techniques:

- `ggplot2`: One of the best packages to visualize data in R is `ggplot2`. It is so popular with the R community that it has almost become an industry standard.
- `GGally`: This is another package that helps visualize data created in a data frame. It includes various plot features such as creating matrix scattered plots.
- `Scatterplot3d`: This package helps create 3D scatter plots, which adds more visualization features.

Creating data reports

Once you have finished exploring the data and you are ready to present your results, you need a way to put your observations, code, and visualizations into a great-looking report.

The following are the list of packages that help us create fascinating reports in R, and it is mandatory that you should install them in your environment:

- `knitr`: The `knitr` package allows us to generate dynamic reports. It also has a lot of other functionalities that make reports easy to read for both technical and non-technical audiences in a wide variety of formats.
- `R Markdown`: The `R Markdown` package allows us to keep text, data, and graphs in one place. It also provides an input to the `knitr` package.

Installing the required R packages and tools

R packages can be installed in two ways: from the Terminal or from inside RStudio. Let's take a look at these.

Installing R packages from the Terminal

To install R packages from the Terminal, follow these steps:

1. Open the Terminal
2. Type and run the following command. Make sure to replace `packagename1` with an actual package name, such as `dplyr`:

```
install.packages("packagename1")
```

Installing R packages from inside RStudio

To install R packages from RStudio, follow these steps:

1. Open **RStudio**
2. Click on **Tools** from the menu bar and then click on **Install Packages...**:

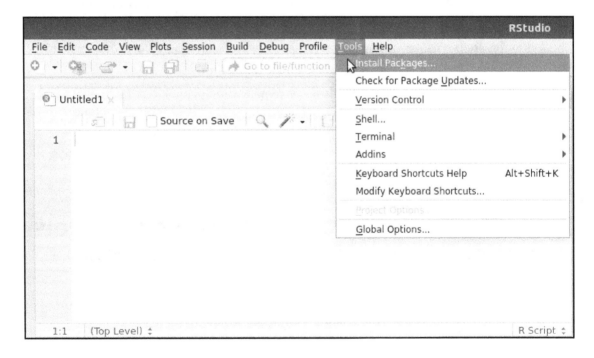

3. In the **Install Packages** dialog box, type in the package name in the **Packages** text box and click on the **Install** button:

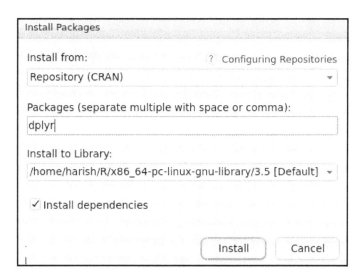

You can also install multiple packages at the same time with both the R command line and RStudio. Just separate the individual packages with commas:

```
install.packages("packagename1", "packagename2")
```

Make sure to install all the packages that are covered in this chapter before proceeding to the next chapter.

Summary

In this chapter, we have learned about the benefits that EDA can bring to businesses across various verticals. We introduced the R packages that will be used in this book to teach concepts related to EDA. We also learned how to set up and install these packages using both the Terminal and RStudio.

The next chapter will demonstrate practical, hands-on code examples that show how to handle reading all kinds of data into R for EDA. We will cover how to use advanced options while importing datasets, including delimited data, Excel data, JSON data, and data from web APIs. We will also look at how to scrape and read in data from the web and how to connect to relational databases from R. We will use R packages such as readr, readxl, jsonlite, httr, rvest, and DBI.

2
Importing Diverse Datasets

This chapter will demonstrate practical, hands-on code examples that show how to handle converting all kinds of data into R for EDA. Here, we will cover how to use advanced options while importing datasets such as delimited data, Excel data, JSON data, and data from web APIs. It will cover the powerful R packages that are needed to work with various data formats.

The following topics will be covered in this chapter:

- Converting all kinds of delimited datasets into R packages using the `readr` package
- Using advanced options for reading in Excel data
- Learning how to use the `jsonlite` package to read JSON in R data structures
- Understanding how to use the `httr` package to read data into R from web APIs
- Getting data into R by scraping the web using the `rvest` package
- Connecting to relational databases from R using the `DBI` package

Technical requirements

You should have hands-on experience or knowledge of the following points before getting started with this book:

- R programming language
- RStudio
- R packages (including `readr`, `readxl`, `jsonlite`, `httr`, `rvest`, `DBI`, `dplyr`, `stringr`, `forcats`, `lubridate`, `hms`, `blob`, `ggplot2`, and `knitr`)

Converting rectangular data into R with the readr R package

Tabular data, or flat rectangular data, comes in many different formats, including CSV and TSV. R's `readr` package provides an easy and flexible way to import all kinds of data into R. It also fails gracefully if there are issues with the data you are trying to import. You can load the `readr` package with the following command:

```
library(readr)
```

The simplest way to import data with `readr` package is to call the specific read data function for different file types, depending on the data you are reading. For example, in the following screenshot, we have a CSV file containing data about automobiles. This data is also bundled as an example dataset with the `readr` package, as shown in the following screenshot:

```
model,mpg,cyl,disp,hp,drat,wt,qsec,vs,am,gear,carb
Mazda RX4,21,6,160,110,3.9,2.62,16.46,0,1,4,4
Mazda RX4 Wag,21,6,160,110,3.9,2.875,17.02,0,1,4,4
Datsun 710,22.8,4,108,93,3.85,2.32,18.61,1,1,4,1
Hornet 4 Drive,21.4,6,258,110,3.08,3.215,19.44,1,0,3,1
Hornet Sportabout,18.7,8,360,175,3.15,3.44,17.02,0,0,3,2
Valiant,18.1,6,225,105,2.76,3.46,20.22,1,0,3,1
Duster 360,14.3,8,360,245,3.21,3.57,15.84,0,0,3,4
Merc 240D,24.4,4,146.7,62,3.69,3.19,20,1,0,4,2
Merc 230,22.8,4,140.8,95,3.92,3.15,22.9,1,0,4,2
Merc 280,19.2,6,167.6,123,3.92,3.44,18.3,1,0,4,4
Merc 280C,17.8,6,167.6,123,3.92,3.44,18.9,1,0,4,4
Merc 450SE,16.4,8,275.8,180,3.07,4.07,17.4,0,0,3,3
Merc 450SL,17.3,8,275.8,180,3.07,3.73,17.6,0,0,3,3
Merc 450SLC,15.2,8,275.8,180,3.07,3.78,18,0,0,3,3
Cadillac Fleetwood,10.4,8,472,205,2.93,5.25,17.98,0,0,3,4
Lincoln Continental,10.4,8,460,215,3,5.424,17.82,0,0,3,4
Chrysler Imperial,14.7,8,440,230,3.23,5.345,17.42,0,0,3,4
Fiat 128,32.4,4,78.7,66,4.08,2.2,19.47,1,1,4,1
Honda Civic,30.4,4,75.7,52,4.93,1.615,18.52,1,1,4,2
Toyota Corolla,33.9,4,71.1,65,4.22,1.835,19.9,1,1,4,1
Toyota Corona,21.5,4,120.1,97,3.7,2.465,20.01,1,0,3,1
Dodge Challenger,15.5,8,318,150,2.76,3.52,16.87,0,0,3,2
AMC Javelin,15.2,8,304,150,3.15,3.435,17.3,0,0,3,2
Camaro Z28,13.3,8,350,245,3.73,3.84,15.41,0,0,3,4
Pontiac Firebird,19.2,8,400,175,3.08,3.845,17.05,0,0,3,2
Fiat X1-9,27.3,4,79,66,4.08,1.935,18.9,1,1,4,1
Porsche 914-2,26,4,120.3,91,4.43,2.14,16.7,0,1,5,2
Lotus Europa,30.4,4,95.1,113,3.77,1.513,16.9,1,1,5,2
Ford Pantera L,15.8,8,351,264,4.22,3.17,14.5,0,1,5,4
Ferrari Dino,19.7,6,145,175,3.62,2.77,15.5,0,1,5,6
Maserati Bora,15,8,301,335,3.54,3.57,14.6,0,1,5,8
Volvo 142E,21.4,4,121,109,4.11,2.78,18.6,1,1,4,2
```

Use the following command to read a particular CSV file in each column:

```
read_csv("mtcars.csv")#> Parsed with column specification:
#> cols(
#>   mpg = col_double(),
```

```
#>    cyl = col_double(),
#>    disp = col_double(),
#>    hp = col_double(),
#>    drat = col_double(),
#>    wt = col_double(),
#>    qsec = col_double(),
#>    vs = col_double(),
#>    am = col_double(),
#>    gear = col_double(),
#>    carb = col_double()
#> )
```

Here, we have a CSV data file. For this, we used the `read_csv` function and passed the file path and name as arguments.

`readr` returns a **tibble** after reading in the data and it also prints the column specifications. Tibbles are data frames that represent values in rows and columns format. Here, we are loading a data file bundled with `readr` by default and saving the tibble in a variable:

```
cars_data <- read_csv(readr_example("mtcars.csv"))
```

The `readr` package is used for reading the data and then it prints the column specifications. This console output is very good for debugging. If you notice any issues with the comma separation, you can always copy and edit the columns in a different call, shown as follows:

```
#> Parsed with column specification:
#> cols(
#>    mpg = col_double(),
#>    cyl = col_double(),
#>    disp = col_double(),
#>    hp = col_double(),
#>    drat = col_double(),
#>    wt = col_double(),
#>    qsec = col_double(),
#>    vs = col_double(),
#>    am = col_double(),
#>    gear = col_double(),
#>    carb = col_double()
#> )
```

The `read_csv` function uses the first line of the CSV file as the column names. However, sometimes, the first few lines of data files contain some extra information and column names start a little down the line. We can use the `skip` parameter to skip the number of lines as follows:

```
read_csv("data.csv", skip = 2)
```

For example, in the preceding code, we skipped the first two lines of the file and asked readr to start reading from the third line.

Sometimes, the data doesn't have column names. We can pass the col_names = FALSE argument to the read_csv function, which specifies to read all the values even if column names are not present:

```
read_csv("data.csv", col_names = FALSE)
```

readr functions support passing in column or specifications to customize the data you are reading. For example, you can specify the type of each column with the col_types argument. Sometimes, it's a good idea to specify the column types because this ensures that there are no errors when reading data:

```
cars_data <- read_csv(readr_example("mtcars.csv"), col_types="ddddddddd")
```

Here, we specified the column type as Double. The following are the column types supported by readr:

- col_logical() [l]: Contains only T, F, TRUE, or FALSE logics
- col_integer() [i]: Integers
- col_double() [d]: Doubles
- col_euro_double() [e]: Euro doubles that use , as the decimal separator
- col_date() [D]: Y-m-d dates
- col_datetime() [T]: ISO 8601 date times
- col_character() [c]: Everything else

There are a lot of other self-explanatory options available when reading data with the read_csv function. For example, a fully loaded read_csv call will look like this:

```
read_csv(file, col_names = TRUE, col_types = NULL,
  locale = default_locale(), na = c("", "NA"), quoted_na = TRUE,
  quote = "\"", comment = "", trim_ws = TRUE, skip = 0,
  n_max = Inf, guess_max = min(1000, n_max),
  progress = show_progress(), skip_empty_rows = TRUE)
```

The following are the parameters used in the preceding code:

- file: This represents the filename
- col_name: This represents the use of column names while reading CSV file
- col_types: This represents the type of column
- locale: This represents which locale should be used

Other parameters used are secondary parameters.

readr read functions

`readr` has six `read` functions that support reading data from six different file formats. These are as follows:

- `read_csv()`: CSV files
- `read_tsv()`: Tab-separated files
- `read_delim()`: General delimited files
- `read_fwf()`: Fixed-width files
- `read_table()`: Tabular files where columns are separated by white-space
- `read_log()`: Web log files

Let's look at an example for each of these packages. We have already had a look at the `read_csv` method. Now let's move on to the `read_tsv` method.

read_tsv method

The `read_tsv` method is quite similar to the `read_csv` method except for the fact that it is used to import tab-separated values. For example, here we have a dataset delimited by tabs:

	mpg	cyl	disp	hp	drat	wt	qsec	vs	am	gear	carb
Mazda RX4	21.0	6	160.0	110	3.90	2.620	16.46	0	1	4	4
Mazda RX4 Wag	21.0	6	160.0	110	3.90	2.875	17.02	0	1	4	4
Datsun 710	22.8	4	108.0	93	3.85	2.320	18.61	1	1	4	1
Hornet 4 Drive	21.4	6	258.0	110	3.08	3.215	19.44	1	0	3	1
Hornet Sportabout	18.7	8	360.0	175	3.15	3.440	17.02	0	0	3	2
Valiant	18.1	6	225.0	105	2.76	3.460	20.22	1	0	3	1
Duster 360	14.3	8	360.0	245	3.21	3.570	15.84	0	0	3	4
Merc 240D	24.4	4	146.7	62	3.69	3.190	20.00	1	0	4	2
Merc 230	22.8	4	140.8	95	3.92	3.150	22.90	1	0	4	2
Merc 280	19.2	6	167.6	123	3.92	3.440	18.30	1	0	4	4

A typical reading of TSV data will look as follows:

```
read_tsv("data.tsv")
```

These are the options for the `read_tsv` function:

```
read_tsv(file, col_names = TRUE, col_types = NULL,
  locale = default_locale(), na = c("", "NA"), quoted_na = TRUE,
  quote = "\"", comment = "", trim_ws = TRUE, skip = 0,
  n_max = Inf, guess_max = min(1000, n_max),
  progress = show_progress(), skip_empty_rows = TRUE)
```

read_delim method

The `read_delim` method is a general case for the `read_csv` or `read_tsv` methods, which are considered as special cases for using this function. The `read_delim` method can be used in cases where you have to read files that are delimited by something other than comma or tab and when there is a need to specify the delimiter explicitly.

For example, here, we have data that is delimited with the | symbol, as shown in the following screenshot:

```
model|mpg|cyl|disp|hp|drat|wt|qsec|vs|am|gear|carb
Mazda RX4|21|6|160|110|3.9|2.62|16.46|0|1|4|4
Mazda RX4 Wag|21|6|160|110|3.9|2.875|17.02|0|1|4|4
Datsun 710|22.8|4|108|93|3.85|2.32|18.61|1|1|4|1
Hornet 4 Drive|21.4|6|258|110|3.08|3.215|19.44|1|0|3|1
Hornet Sportabout|18.7|8|360|175|3.15|3.44|17.02|0|0|3|2
Valiant|18.1|6|225|105|2.76|3.46|20.22|1|0|3|1
Duster 360|14.3|8|360|245|3.21|3.57|15.84|0|0|3|4
Merc 240D|24.4|4|146.7|62|3.69|3.19|20|1|0|4|2
Merc 230|22.8|4|140.8|95|3.92|3.15|22.9|1|0|4|2
Merc 280|19.2|6|167.6|123|3.92|3.44|18.3|1|0|4|4
Merc 280C|17.8|6|167.6|123|3.92|3.44|18.9|1|0|4|4
Merc 450SE|16.4|8|275.8|180|3.07|4.07|17.4|0|0|3|3
Merc 450SL|17.3|8|275.8|180|3.07|3.73|17.6|0|0|3|3
Merc 450SLC|15.2|8|275.8|180|3.07|3.78|18|0|0|3|3
Cadillac Fleetwood|10.4|8|472|205|2.93|5.25|17.98|0|0|3|4
Lincoln Continental|10.4|8|460|215|3|5.424|17.82|0|0|3|4
Chrysler Imperial|14.7|8|440|230|3.23|5.345|17.42|0|0|3|4
Fiat 128|32.4|4|78.7|66|4.08|2.2|19.47|1|1|4|1
Honda Civic|30.4|4|75.7|52|4.93|1.615|18.52|1|1|4|2
Toyota Corolla|33.9|4|71.1|65|4.22|1.835|19.9|1|1|4|1
Toyota Corona|21.5|4|120.1|97|3.7|2.465|20.01|1|0|3|1
Dodge Challenger|15.5|8|318|150|2.76|3.52|16.87|0|0|3|2
AMC Javelin|15.2|8|304|150|3.15|3.435|17.3|0|0|3|2
Camaro Z28|13.3|8|350|245|3.73|3.84|15.41|0|0|3|4
Pontiac Firebird|19.2|8|400|175|3.08|3.845|17.05|0|0|3|2
Fiat X1-9|27.3|4|79|66|4.08|1.935|18.9|1|1|4|1
Porsche 914-2|26|4|120.3|91|4.43|2.14|16.7|0|1|5|2
Lotus Europa|30.4|4|95.1|113|3.77|1.513|16.9|1|1|5|2
Ford Pantera L|15.8|8|351|264|4.22|3.17|14.5|0|1|5|4
Ferrari Dino|19.7|6|145|175|3.62|2.77|15.5|0|1|5|6
Maserati Bora|15|8|301|335|3.54|3.57|14.6|0|1|5|8
Volvo 142E|21.4|4|121|109|4.11|2.78|18.6|1|1|4|2
```

We can read this data by specifying an explicit delimiter here by using the
`delim` argument:

```
read_delim("data.del", delim = "|")
```

read_fwf method

The `read_fwf` method is used to read data from fixed width files, where every field is in
the same place in every line. The default usage will be to read the data in text format in the
R workspace. The code for this is shown as follows:

```
read_fwf("data.txt")
```

Here, `readr` will try to guess the column widths. However, to avoid errors, you could also
specify column widths explicitly as follows:

```
read_fwf(data.txt, fwf_widths(c(10, 20, 18), c("ID", "Revenue", "Region")))
```

read_table method

If you have text files with tabular data that you read and the columns are separated by one
or more columns of space, then `read_table` is the method to use:

```
read_table("table.csv")
```

There are two versions of this method:

- `read_table()`: This should be used when each line of data is of the same length
  and each column is in the same position
- `read_table2()`: This is more flexible in terms of line length and column
  position

read_log method

The `read_log` method is used for reading standard formats of log file data into R. For example, log files are shown in the following screenshot:

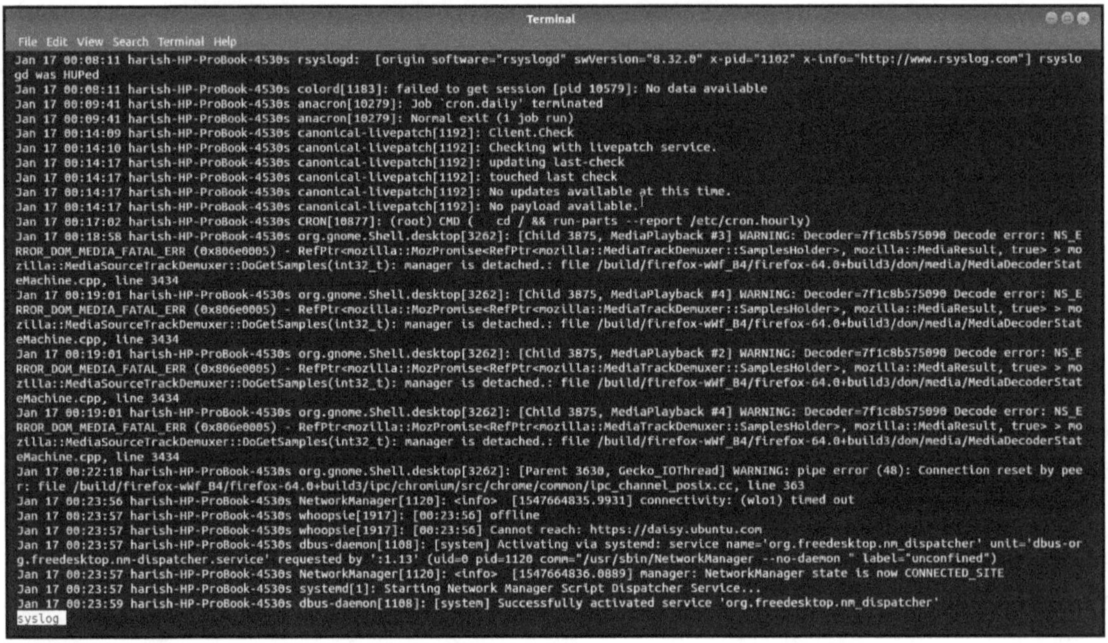

The most straightforward way to include log files in the R workspace is to pass the log filename to the `read_log` method:

```
read_log("data.log")
```

The `read_log` method returns a tibble from the log data:

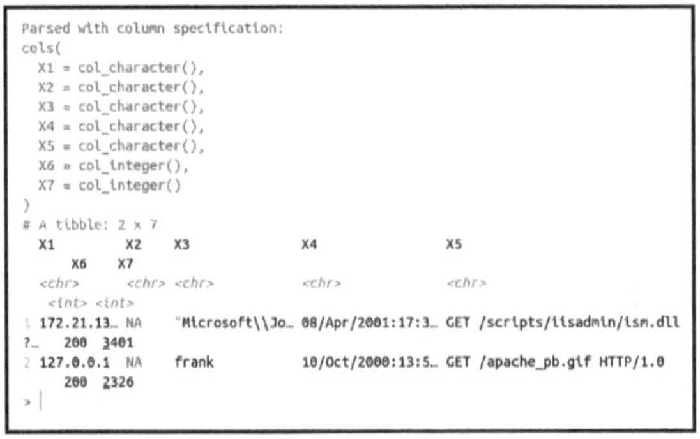

Reading in Excel data with the readxl R package

The `readxl` R package makes it very easy and straightforward to read data from Excel files into R:

A1				f_x Σ =	model							
	A	B	C	D	E	F	G	H	I	J	K	L
1	model	mpg	cyl	disp	hp	drat	wt	qsec	vs	am	gear	carb
2	Mazda RX4	21	6	160	110	3.9	2.62	16.46	0	1	4	4
3	Mazda RX4 Wag	21	6	160	110	3.9	2.875	17.02	0	1	4	4
4	Datsun 710	22.8	4	108	93	3.85	2.32	18.61	1	1	4	1
5	Hornet 4 Drive	21.4	6	258	110	3.08	3.215	19.44	1	0	3	1
6	Hornet Sportabout	18.7	8	360	175	3.15	3.44	17.02	0	0	3	2
7	Valiant	18.1	6	225	105	2.76	3.46	20.22	1	0	3	1
8	Duster 360	14.3	8	360	245	3.21	3.57	15.84	0	0	3	4
9	Merc 240D	24.4	4	146.7	62	3.69	3.19	20	1	0	4	2
10	Merc 230	22.8	4	140.8	95	3.92	3.15	22.9	1	0	4	2
11	Merc 280	19.2	6	167.6	123	3.92	3.44	18.3	1	0	4	4
12	Merc 280C	17.8	6	167.6	123	3.92	3.44	18.9	1	0	4	4
13	Merc 450SE	16.4	8	275.8	180	3.07	4.07	17.4	0	0	3	3
14	Merc 450SL	17.3	8	275.8	180	3.07	3.73	17.6	0	0	3	3
15	Merc 450SLC	15.2	8	275.8	180	3.07	3.78	18	0	0	3	3
16	Cadillac Fleetwood	10.4	8	472	205	2.93	5.25	17.98	0	0	3	4
17	Lincoln Continental	10.4	8	460	215	3	5.424	17.82	0	0	3	4
18	Chrysler Imperial	14.7	8	440	230	3.23	5.345	17.42	0	0	3	4
19	Fiat 128	32.4	4	78.7	66	4.08	2.2	19.47	1	1	4	1
20	Honda Civic	30.4	4	75.7	52	4.93	1.615	18.52	1	1	4	2
21	Toyota Corolla	33.9	4	71.1	65	4.22	1.835	19.9	1	1	4	1
22	Toyota Corona	21.5	4	120.1	97	3.7	2.465	20.01	1	0	3	1
23	Dodge Challenger	15.5	8	318	150	2.76	3.52	16.87	0	0	3	2
24	AMC Javelin	15.2	8	304	150	3.15	3.435	17.3	0	0	3	2
25	Camaro Z28	13.3	8	350	245	3.73	3.84	15.41	0	0	3	4
26	Pontiac Firebird	19.2	8	400	175	3.08	3.845	17.05	0	0	3	2
27	Fiat X1-9	27.3	4	79	66	4.08	1.935	18.9	1	1	4	1
28	Porsche 914-2	26	4	120.3	91	4.43	2.14	16.7	0	1	5	2
29	Lotus Europa	30.4	4	95.1	113	3.77	1.513	16.9	1	1	5	2

|◄ ◄ ► ►| ✚ | mtcars

We start by loading the module into R:

```
library(readxl)
```

Reading Excel data with `readxl` is simple; we just need to call the `read_excel` function and pass in the file path, as follows:

```
read_excel("data.xls")
```

`readxl` supports both the old XLS and the new XLSX format. It guesses the format from the extension of the file being read:

```
read_excel("data.xlsx")
```

Excel files sometimes have multiple sheets. For example, the following Excel file has multiple sheets:

You can easily handle them with the `readxl` package. To see the number of sheets in the Excel document, use the `excel_sheets` command:

```
excel_sheets("data.xlsx")
#1> [i] "sheet1" "sheet2"
```

We can also specify which sheet should be accessed by using `read_excel` with the `sheet` argument:

```
read_excel("data.xlsx", sheet= 1)
```

To access a particular sheet of Excel, the `sheet` parameter is used:

```
read_excel("data.xlsx", sheet= "sheet1")
```

Reading in JSON data with the jsonlite R package

`jsonlite` is a JSON data parser for R. It makes reading data from JSON sources really easy and efficient.

Loading the jsonlite package

The following command is executed to include the `jsonlite` package in the R workspace:

```
library(jsonlite)
```

Data processing or parsing is done through a process called **simplification**. This is where JSON arrays are converted from a list into a more specific R class. Basically, with a simplification process, the arrays are broken down into values that can be easily understood. There are three different options that can be passed as arguments to the `fromJSON` function:

- `simplifyVector`: This option is used to convert arrays into a vector format
- `simplifyDataFrame`: This option is used to convert arrays into a data frame format with representation of rows and columns
- `simplifyMatrix`: This is similar to the data frame format, the only difference being that data should be included as a numeric representation

Let's look at an example of a data frame:

```
json_data <-
'[
  {"Name" : "John", "Age" : 42, "City" : "New York"},
  {"Name" : "Jane", "Age" : 41, "City" : "Paris"},
  {},
  {"Name" : "Bob", "City" : "London"}
]'
df <- fromJSON(json_data)
df
```

Here, `json_data` key values are converted into a data frame.

Getting data into R from web APIs using the httr R package

We need to implement the following steps to extract data using the `httr` package in R workspace:

First, we load the `httr` package:

```
library(httr)
```

We then call GET function and pass it as a URL:

```
r <- GET("http://httpbin.org/get")
```

This gives us a response object that can be processed further for data. To start with, we can print out the response object to get some information about the data:

```
>r
Response [http://httpbin.org/get]
  Date: 2019-01-18 03:45
  Status: 200
  Content-Type: application/json
  Size: 326 B
{
  "args": {},
  "headers": {
    "Accept": "application/json, text/xml, application/xml, */*",
    "Accept-Encoding": "gzip, deflate",
    "Connection": "close",
    "Host": "httpbin.org",
    "User-Agent": "libcurl/7.58.0 r-curl/3.2 httr/1.3.1"
  },
  "origin": "106.200.254.84",
...
```

We can get to the data contained in the response using the `content` method. For example, to get the body of the request as a raw vector, the following command is executed:

```
> content(r, "raw")
  [1] 7b 0a 20 20 22 61 72 67 73 22 3a 20 7b 7d 2c 20 0a 20 20 22 68 65 61
64 65 72 73 22 3a 20
 [31] 7b 0a 20 20 20 20 22 41 63 63 65 70 74 22 3a 20 22 61 70 70 6c 69 63
61 74 69 6f 6e 2f 6a
 [61] 73 6f 6e 2c 20 74 65 78 74 2f 78 6d 6c 2c 20 61 70 70 6c 69 63 61 74
69 6f 6e 2f 78 6d 6c
 [91] 2c 20 2a 2f 2a 22 2c 20 0a 20 20 20 20 22 41 63 63 65 70 74 2d 45 6e
```

```
63 6f 64 69 6e 67 22
[121] 3a 20 22 67 7a 69 70 2c 20 64 65 66 6c 61 74 65 22 2c 20 0a 20 20 20
20 22 43 6f 6e 6e 65
[151] 63 74 69 6f 6e 22 3a 20 22 63 6c 6f 73 65 22 2c 20 0a 20 20 20 20 22
48 6f 73 74 22 3a 20
[181] 22 68 74 74 70 62 69 6e 2e 6f 72 67 22 2c 20 0a 20 20 20 20 22 55 73
65 72 2d 41 67 65 6e
[211] 74 22 3a 20 22 6c 69 62 63 75 72 6c 2f 37 2e 35 38 2e 30 20 72 2d 63
75 72 6c 2f 33 2e 32
[241] 20 68 74 74 72 2f 31 2e 33 2e 31 22 0a 20 20 7d 2c 20 0a 20 20 22 6f
72 69 67 69 6e 22 3a
[271] 20 22 31 30 36 2e 32 30 30 2e 32 35 34 2e 38 34 22 2c 20 0a 20 20 22
75 72 6c 22 3a 20 22
[301] 68 74 74 70 3a 2f 2f 68 74 74 70 62 69 6e 2e 6f 72 67 2f 67 65 74 22
0a 7d 0a
>
```

In the next section, we will learn to get data into R by scraping the web using the `rvest` package.

Getting data into R by scraping the web using the rvest package

In this section, we will focus on **web scraping** and how to implement it using the `rvest` package.

Web scraping is the procedure of converting unstructured data into a structured format. Structured data can be easily accessed and used. We will use R for scraping the data of most popular feature films from the IMDb website.

The following steps are implemented to get data into R using the `rvest` package:

1. Install the `rvest` package. It is mandatory to install it, as it does not come as a built-in library:

   ```
   > install.packages('rvest')
   package 'rvest' successfully unpacked and MD5 sums checked The
   downloaded binary packages are in
   C:\Users\Radhika\AppData\Local\Temp\RtmpMvNUA5\downloaded_packages
   ```

2. Include the installed package in R's workspace:

   ```
   > library(rvest)
   ```

3. Let's start web scraping the IMDb website, which displays the most popular feature films in a given year:

```
> url <-
'https://www.imdb.com/search/title?count=100&release_date=2017,2017
&title_type=feature'> #Reading html code from mentioned url>
webpage <- read_html(url)> webpage{xml_document}<html
xmlns:og="http://ogp.me/ns#"
xmlns:fb="http://www.facebook.com/2008/fbml">[1] <head>\n<meta
http-equiv="Content-Type" content="text/html;
charset=UTF-8">\n<script type="text/ ...[2] <body id="styleguide-
v2" class="fixed">\n\n <img height="1" width="1" style="display:
...
```

4. As you can see, there are various CSS selectors that can be used to scrape the required data:

```
> #Using CSS selectors to scrap the rankings section>
rank_data_html <- html_nodes(webpage,'.text-primary')>
rank_data_html{xml_nodeset (100)} [1] <span class="lister-item-
index unbold text-primary">1.</span> [2] <span class="lister-item-
index unbold text-primary">2.</span> [3] <span class="lister-item-
index unbold text-primary">3.</span> [4] <span class="lister-item-
index unbold text-primary">4.</span> [5] <span class="lister-item-
index unbold text-primary">5.</span> [6] <span class="lister-item-
index unbold text-primary">6.</span> [7] <span class="lister-item-
index unbold text-primary">7.</span> [8] <span class="lister-item-
index unbold text-primary">8.</span> [9] <span class="lister-item-
index unbold text-primary">9.</span>[10] <span class="lister-item-
index unbold text-primary">10.</span>[11] <span class="lister-item-
index unbold text-primary">11.</span>[12] <span class="lister-item-
index unbold text-primary">12.</span>[13] <span class="lister-item-
index unbold text-primary">13.</span>[14] <span class="lister-item-
index unbold text-primary">14.</span>[15] <span class="lister-item-
index unbold text-primary">15.</span>[16] <span class="lister-item-
index unbold text-primary">16.</span>[17] <span class="lister-item-
index unbold text-primary">17.</span>[18] <span class="lister-item-
index unbold text-primary">18.</span>[19] <span class="lister-item-
index unbold text-primary">19.</span>[20] <span class="lister-item-
index unbold text-primary">20.</span>...
```

5. Use the following code to get the specific rank of each film:

```
> rank_data <- html_text(rank_data_html)> head(rank_data)[1] "1."
"2." "3." "4." "5." "6."
```

In the next section, we will focus more on importing the data into R from databases using the required package.

Importing data into R from relational databases using the DBI R package

Database Independent Interface (**DBI**) makes connecting to and getting data from various relational databases from R very easy and efficient.

To use DBI, we load `DBI` first:

```
library(DBI)
```

We then create an in-memory `RSQLite` database:

```
con <- dbConnect(RSQLite::SQLite(), dbname = ":memory:")
```

We can print a list of tables as follows:

```
dbListTables(con)
```

Summary

In this chapter, we listed some of the various packages that are available for converting various kinds of data into R. There are a lot of different options, and even the options we have listed have a wide functionality, which we are going to cover and use as we go further into the book. We learned how to read all kinds of delimited datasets into R packages using the `readr` package and also advanced options for reading in Excel data. We then learned how to use the `jsonlite` package to read JSON in R data structures and learned how to use the `httr` package to read data into R from web APIs.

At the end of the chapter, we learned how to get data into R by scraping the web using the `rvest` package, and we also learned how to connect to relational databases from R using the DBI package.

In the next chapter, we will explore how to identify and clean missing and erroneous data. This will cover concepts such as data manipulation, wrangling, and reshaping. The chapter also includes various filtering methods and package implementations with diagrams.

3
Examining, Cleaning, and Filtering

This chapter will introduce you to techniques to identify and clean missing and erroneous data formats. Concepts such as data manipulation, wrangling, and reshaping will be covered in this chapter. We will also learn how to select and filter data along with handling time series and textual data. These methods will be demonstrated using R packages such as `dplyr`, `tidyr`, `stringr`, `forcats`, `lubridate`, `hms`, and `blob`.

In this chapter, we will be covering the following topics:

- Reshaping and tidying up missing and erroneous data
- Manipulating and mutating data
- Selecting and filtering data
- Cleaning and manipulating time series data
- Handling complex textual data

Technical requirements

You should have hands-on experience or knowledge of the following points before getting started with this chapter:

- R programming language
- RStudio
- R packages
  (including `readr`, `readxl`, `jsonlite`, `httr`, `rvest`, `DBI`, `dplyr`, `stringr`, `forcats`, `lubridate`, `hms`, `blob`, `ggplot2`, and `knitr`)

About the dataset

The dataset that we will be focusing on throughout this chapter is the `Auto.MPG` dataset, which is used predominantly with the R language. This dataset gives the complete details of fuel economy data for the years 1999 and 2008 for 38 popular car models. This dataset also comes with the `ggplot2` package, which we will cover in the coming chapters.

For now, we will focus on importing the dataset from the CSV file, which you can download from the following link:

`https://github.com/PacktPublishing/Hands-On-Exploratory-Data-Analysis-with-R/tree/master/ch03`

For more details pertaining to the dataset, you can refer to the following link:

`https://archive.ics.uci.edu/ml/datasets/auto+mpg`

Once the download is complete, we can import the CSV file into the dataset. With this conversion, we can include the dataset in the R workspace:

```
> mpg <-read.csv("highway_mpg.csv", stringsAsFactors = FALSE)
> View(mpg)
```

From this, we get the following output:

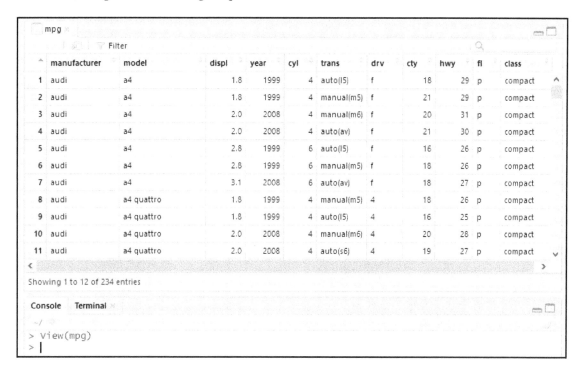

As shown in the preceding screenshot, the Auto.MPG dataset includes various attributes, as follows:

Name	Abbreviated form
Manufacturers	Manufacturer
Model manufactured	Model
Displacement	Displ
Year of manufacturing	Year
Cylinders	Cyl
Transmission types	Trans
Drive versus cylinder	Drv
Displacement versus highway efficiency	Hwy
Fuel types	Fl
Vehicle class	Class

The dataset, which is represented in tabular format, is as follows:

	manufacturer	model	displ	year	cyl	trans	drv	cty	hwy	fl	class
1	audi	a4	1.8	1999	4	auto(l5)	f	18	29	p	compact
2	audi	a4	1.8	1999	4	manual(m5)	f	21	29	p	compact
3	audi	a4	2.0	2008	4	manual(m6)	f	20	31	p	compact
4	audi	a4	2.0	2008	4	auto(av)	f	21	30	p	compact
5	audi	a4	2.8	1999	6	auto(l5)	f	16	26	p	compact
6	audi	a4	2.8	1999	6	manual(m5)	f	18	26	p	compact
7	audi	a4	3.1	2008	6	auto(av)	f	18	27	p	compact
8	audi	a4 quattro	1.8	1999	4	manual(m5)	4	18	26	p	compact
9	audi	a4 quattro	1.8	1999	4	auto(l5)	4	16	25	p	compact
10	audi	a4 quattro	2.0	2008	4	manual(m6)	4	20	28	p	compact
11	audi	a4 quattro	2.0	2008	4	auto(s6)	4	19	27	p	compact
12	audi	a4 quattro	2.8	1999	6	auto(l5)	4	15	25	p	compact

Showing 1 to 12 of 234 entries

The description, including data types for each attribute of the dataset, can be achieved with the following command:

```
> str(mpg)
'data.frame':  234 obs. of  11 variables:
 $ manufacturer: chr  "audi" "audi"    "audi" "audi" ...
 $ model       : chr  "a4" "a4"    "a4" "a4" ...
 $ displ       : num  1.8 1.8 2 2 2.8 2.8    3.1 1.8 1.8 2 ...
 $ year        : int  1999 1999 2008 2008    1999 1999 2008 1999 1999 2008
...
 $ cyl         : int  4 4 4 4 6 6 6 4 4 4    ...
 $ trans       : chr  "auto(l5)"    "manual(m5)" "manual(m6)" "auto(av)" ...
 $ drv         : chr  "f" "f"    "f" "f" ...
 $ cty         : int  18 21 20 21 16 18    18 18 16 20 ...
 $ hwy         : int  29 29 31 30 26 26    27 26 25 28 ...
 $ fl          : chr  "p" "p"    "p" "p" ...
 $ class       : chr  "compact"    "compact" "compact" "compact" ...
```

The `str` function is declared as an alternative to the `summary` function. It displays the internal structure of an R object in a compact manner.

Reshaping and tidying up erroneous data

Erroneous data is regarded as data that falls outside of what is accepted and what should be rejected by the system. In this section, we will focus on two major activities: reshaping and tidying up erroneous data. With the R programming language, this process can be achieved with the `tidyr` package. This package is designed specifically for data tidying and works well with manipulated data. It is important that you install this package if you have newly installed the R environment.

The following steps are implemented to include this package in the R environment:

1. Use the `install.packages` command to install the `tidyr` package in its entirety:

   ```
   > install.packages("tidyr")
   ```

   From this, we get the following output:

   ```
   > install.packages("tidyr")
   Installing package into 'C:/Users/Radhika/Documents/R/win-library/3.5'
   (as 'lib' is unspecified)
   trying URL 'https://cran.rstudio.com/bin/windows/contrib/3.5/tidyr_0.8.3.zip'
   Content type 'application/zip' length 953866 bytes (931 KB)
   downloaded 931 KB

   package 'tidyr' successfully unpacked and MD5 sums checked

   The downloaded binary packages are in
           C:\Users\Radhika\AppData\Local\Temp\Rtmpgt3r8E\downloaded_packages
   ```

2. Now, it is important to include this package in your workspace (R environment). By including it, we can call the necessary libraries and functions associated with this package in the R workspace:

   ```
   > library(tidyr)
   ```

From this, we get the following output:

```
Console    Terminal  ⌐
~/ ⌐
> library(tidyr)

Attaching package: 'tidyr'

The following object is masked _by_ '.GlobalEnv':

    who

The following object is masked from 'package:Matrix':

    expand

Warning message:
package 'tidyr' was built under R version 3.5.3
> |
```

Once we have included the `tidyr` package in our system, we can proceed with reshaping and tidying up the `mpg` dataset. This process requires the following functions:

- `gather()`
- `unite()`
- `separate()`
- `spread()`

The gather() function

There are times when our data is considered raw and unstacked (not in chronological order) and a common attribute of concern is used across the columns. To reformat the data so that these common attributes take up a single variable, the `gather ()` function will take multiple columns and break them into key-value pairs, duplicating all other columns if needed.

The following illustration will help us to better understand the implementation of `gather()` function. The syntax for implementing the `gather()` function is as follows:

```
gather(data, key, value, ..., na.rm =    FALSE, convert = FALSE)
```

Here, the parameters of the function are as follows:

- `data`: Data frame
- `key`: Name of the key
- `value`: Name of the value
- `na.rm`: If TRUE, it will remove rows from the output
- `convert`: If TRUE, it will automatically convert the specified key column

Suppose we need to gather information relating to the manufacturer and model and display other attributes in same way. In this case, there is a need to present only manufacturers and models in a systematic manner. We can achieve this with the help of the `gather()` function, demonstrated as follows:

```
> mpg2 <- mpg %>% gather(mpg, "Year   of Establishment", "year", -
manufacturer)
> View(mpg2)
```

The output generated is displayed as follows:

	manufacturer	model	displ	cyl	trans	drv	cty	hwy	fl	class	mpg	Year of Establishment
4	audi	a4	2.0	4	auto(av)	f	21	30	p	compact	year	2008
5	audi	a4	2.8	6	auto(l5)	f	16	26	p	compact	year	1999
6	audi	a4	2.8	6	manual(m5)	f	18	26	p	compact	year	1999
7	audi	a4	3.1	6	auto(av)	f	18	27	p	compact	year	2008
8	audi	a4 quattro	1.8	4	manual(m5)	4	18	26	p	compact	year	1999
9	audi	a4 quattro	1.8	4	auto(l5)	4	16	25	p	compact	year	1999
10	audi	a4 quattro	2.0	4	manual(m6)	4	20	20	p	compact	year	2008
11	audi	a4 quattro	2.0	4	auto(s6)	4	19	27	p	compact	year	2008
12	audi	a4 quattro	2.8	6	auto(l5)	4	15	25	p	compact	year	1999
13	audi	a4 quattro	2.8	6	manual(m5)	4	17	25	p	compact	year	1999
14	audi	a4 quattro	3.1	6	auto(s6)	4	17	25	p	compact	year	2008

It is clearly visible that the key-value pair is generated for the year of establishment of each and every model included in the dataset.

The unite() function

unite focuses on combining multiple columns into a single column. This is regarded as a convenience function that pastes multiple columns together.

The basic implementation syntax is as follows:

```
unite(data, col,  ..., sep = "_",    remove = TRUE)
```

Here, the parameters are as follows:

- data: Data frame.
- col: The name of the column to be added. Further specification of columns can be added.
- sep: Separator to use between the values.
- remove: If TRUE, this will remove input columns from the data frame mentioned.

In our dataset, where we need to combine Fuel Type columns and Drive versus Cylinder attributes to understand the fuel efficiency, we can use the unite function with a separator value to combine the columns:

```
> mpg4<- unite_(mpg, "FuelEfficiency", c("drv","fl"))
> View(mpg4)
```

The output generated is as follows:

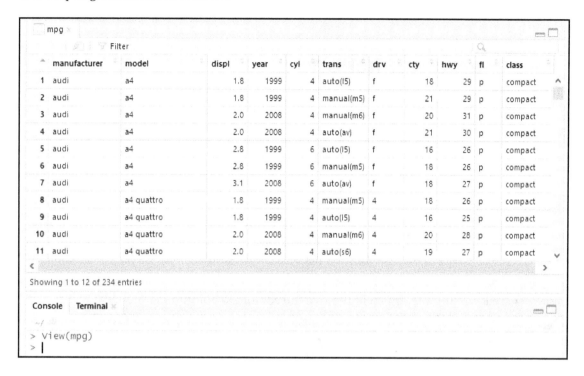

mpg4 is a new dataset created as follows:

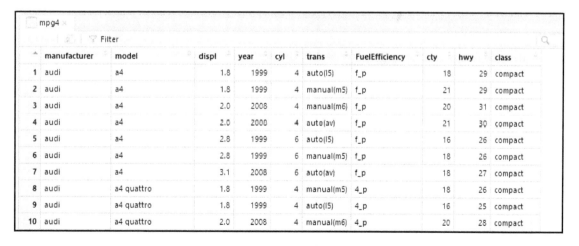

FuelEfficiency is the column that combines both attributes with a separator, _.

We can combine multiple columns together as one in a similar fashion, with the main focus being to tidy up the data.

The separate() function

This function works in a reverse manner to the `unite()` function. It separates a single column into multiple columns for the dataset mentioned.

The syntax for implementing the `separate()` function is as follows:

```
separate(data, col, into, sep = "[^[:alnum:]]+",    remove = TRUE,
   convert = FALSE")
```

Here, the parameters are as follows:

- `data`: Data frame
- `col`: Refers to the column that needs to be separated
- `sep`: The separator used, if any
- `remove`: If `TRUE`, this will remove the combined column mentioned
- `convert`: If `TRUE`, this will convert the column to the specified type

We can create a reverse scenario for the example mentioned in the `unite()` function. The `FuelEfficiency` column can be separated from the original ones using the following command:

```
> mpg3<- mpg4 %>% separate(FuelEfficiency, c("drv", "f1"))
> View(mpg3)
```

The output generated is as follows:

	manufacturer	model	displ	year	cyl	trans	drv	f1	cty	hwy	class
1	audi	a4	1.8	1999	4	auto(l5)	f	p	18	29	compact
2	audi	a4	1.8	1999	4	manual(m5)	f	p	21	29	compact
3	audi	a4	2.0	2008	4	manual(m6)	f	p	20	31	compact
4	audi	a4	2.0	2008	4	auto(av)	f	p	21	30	compact
5	audi	a4	2.8	1999	6	auto(l5)	f	p	16	26	compact
6	audi	a4	2.8	1999	6	manual(m5)	f	p	18	26	compact
7	audi	a4	3.1	2008	6	auto(av)	f	p	18	27	compact
8	audi	a4 quattro	1.8	1999	4	manual(m5)	4	p	18	26	compact
9	audi	a4 quattro	1.8	1999	4	auto(l5)	4	p	16	25	compact
10	audi	a4 quattro	2.0	2008	4	manual(m6)	4	p	20	28	compact

The spread() function

The `spread()` function spreads the key-value pair across multiple columns of the dataset mentioned.

The syntax of the `spread()` function is as follows:

```
spread(data, key, value, fill = NA,   convert = FALSE, drop = TRUE,
  sep = NULL)
```

Here, the parameters are as follows:

- `data`: Data frame
- `key, value`: Refers to the key-value pair that will be generated

The other parameters are secondary parameters.

Manipulating and mutating data

In this section, we will focus on the way in which the `dplyr` package works, which helps the manipulation and mutation of data. This package primarily provides a flexible grammar for data manipulation. It is the next iteration of the `plyr` package, which focuses on tools for working with data frames.

The following steps are implemented to include this package in the R environment:

1. Use the `install.packages` command to install the `dplyr` package in its entirety:

   ```
   > install.packages("dplyr")
   ```

   If the package is already in use, it will be reinstalled or will prompt with the following message:

   ```
   > install.packages("dplyr")
   Installing package into 'C:/Users/Radhika/Documents/R/win-library/3.5'
   (as 'lib' is unspecified)
   warning in install.packages :
     package 'dplyr' is in use and will not be installed
   >
   ```

2. Now, it is important to include this package in your workspace (R environment). By including it, we can call the necessary libraries and functions associated with this package in the R workspace:

```
> library(dplyr)
```

The command execution in the R workspace or platform is depicted in the following screenshot:

The preceding package has a set of functions or *verbs* that execute several data manipulation operations. These operations include selecting specific columns, adding new columns, filtering rows, ordering the row pattern, and summarizing the data. dplyr is known to be a powerful R package that is used for the transformation and summarization of tabular data frames with the structure of defined columns and rows.

Now, we will focus on mutation and manipulation of the Auto.MPG dataset with the help of this package.

The various functions that will be implemented are as follows:

- mutate()
- summarise()
- group_by()
- glimpse()
- arrange()

The mutate() function

The mutate() function is used to add new columns to the dataset mentioned. It is considered useful to create attributes with respect to functions of other attributes in the dataset. The mutate() function is regarded as one of the essential tools for new feature creation, especially during the data preprocessing stage.

We have numeric columns in our dataset. Consider a scenario where we have to create a column to calculate the displacement and number of cylinders used for covering a certain distance. We can implement the `mutate()` function to achieve this:

```
> mpgMutate <- mpg %>% mutate(nv=cyl+displ)
> View(mpgMutate)
```

The output with the new value of the `nv` attribute is displayed as follows, and includes a summation of the `cyl` and `displ` attributes:

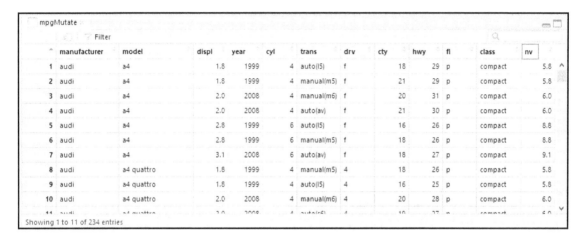

The group_by() function

The `group_by()` function is used to group data together based on one or more columns. It works in a similar fashion to the GROUP BY clause of **Structured Query Language** (**SQL**).

Consider that we need to create a dataset that groups the columns according to model names. This can be achieved using the `group_by()` function, as follows:

```
> mpgGroupBy <- mpg %>%group_by(model)
> View(mpgGroupBy)
```

We get the following output:

	manufacturer	model	displ	year	cyl	trans	drv	cty	hwy	fl	class
1	audi	a4	1.8	1999	4	auto(l5)	f	18	29	p	compact
2	audi	a4	1.8	1999	4	manual(m5)	f	21	29	p	compact
3	audi	a4	2.0	2008	4	manual(m6)	f	20	31	p	compact
4	audi	a4	2.0	2008	4	auto(av)	f	21	30	p	compact
5	audi	a4	2.8	1999	6	auto(l5)	f	16	26	p	compact
6	audi	a4	2.8	1999	6	manual(m5)	f	18	26	p	compact
7	audi	a4	3.1	2008	6	auto(av)	f	18	27	p	compact
8	audi	a4 quattro	1.8	1999	4	manual(m5)	4	18	26	p	compact
9	audi	a4 quattro	1.8	1999	4	auto(l5)	4	16	25	p	compact
10	audi	a4 quattro	2.0	2008	4	manual(m6)	4	20	28	p	compact
11	audi	a4 quattro	2.0	2008	4	auto(s6)	4	19	27	p	compact
12	audi	a4 quattro	2.8	1999	6	auto(l5)	4	15	25	p	compact

Showing 1 to 12 of 234 entries

The summarize() function

The `summarize()` function is used to aggregate multiple column values to a single column. It is predominantly used with the `group_by()` function.

Consider a scenario in which we want to summarize the data as per the displacement covered by the automobiles. In this case, the following command can be executed with a combination of the `group_by()` and `summarize()` functions:

```
> mpgSummarize<- mpg %>% group_by(displ) %>%
summarize(avg_displ=mean(displ))
> mpgSummarize
# A tibble: 35 x 2
   displ avg_displ
   <dbl> <dbl>
 1 1.6 1.6
 2 1.8 1.8
 3 1.9 1.9
 4 2   2
 5 2.2 2.2
 6 2.4 2.4
 7 2.5 2.5
 8 2.7 2.7
 9 2.8 2.8
```

```
10 3 3
# ... with 25 more rows
> View(mpgSummarize)
```

The following table gives summarized details relating to displacement and the average displacement to be calculated:

	displ	avg_displ
1	1.6	1.6
2	1.8	1.8
3	1.9	1.9
4	2.0	2.0
5	2.2	2.2
6	2.4	2.4
7	2.5	2.5
8	2.7	2.7
9	2.8	2.8
10	3.0	3.0
11	3.1	3.1
12	3.3	3.3

The arrange() function

The arrange() function is used to sort the columns of a dataset in an ascending or descending order and the default is considered as the ascending order. The working pattern is the same as the ORDER BY clause of SQL.

Our dataset includes details of the model as per the launch year, and now we need to arrange these details according to the year of establishment, which can be achieved as follows:

```
> mpgArrange<- mpg %>%arrange(mpg$year)
> View(mpgArrange)
```

The reordering pattern according to the year is depicted properly in the following screenshot:

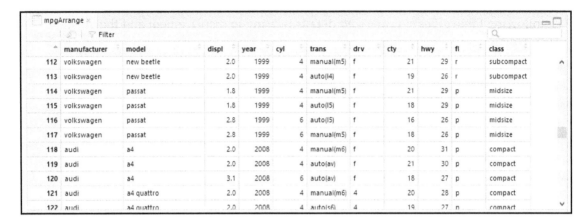

The glimpse() function

The `glimpse()` function of the `dplyr` package can be used to see the columns of the dataset and display some portion of the data with respect to each attribute that can fit on a single line.

We can apply this function to get a glimpse of our `mpg` dataset:

```
> glimpse(mpg)
```

We get the following output for the preceding code:

```
> glimpse(mpg)
Observations: 234
variables: 11
$ manufacturer <chr> "audi", "audi", "audi", "audi", "audi", "audi", "audi", "audi", "audi", "audi", "audi...
$ model        <chr> "a4", "a4", "a4", "a4", "a4", "a4", "a4", "a4 quattro", "a4 quattro", "a4 quattro", "...
$ displ        <dbl> 1.8, 1.8, 2.0, 2.0, 2.8, 2.8, 3.1, 1.8, 1.8, 2.0, 2.0, 2.8, 2.8, 3.1, 3.1, 2.8, 3.1, ...
$ year         <int> 1999, 1999, 2008, 2008, 1999, 1999, 2008, 1999, 1999, 2008, 2008, 1999, 1999, 2008, 2...
$ cyl          <int> 4, 4, 4, 4, 6, 6, 6, 4, 4, 4, 4, 6, 6, 6, 6, 8, 8, 8, 8, 8, 8, 8, 8, 8, 8, 8, 8, 8...
$ trans        <chr> "auto(l5)", "manual(m5)", "manual(m6)", "auto(av)", "auto(l5)", "manual(m5)", "auto(a...
$ drv          <chr> "f", "f", "f", "f", "f", "f", "f", "4", "4", "4", "4", "4", "4", "4", "4", "4", "4", ...
$ cty          <int> 18, 21, 20, 21, 16, 18, 18, 18, 16, 20, 19, 15, 17, 17, 15, 15, 17, 16, 14, 11, 14, 1...
$ hwy          <int> 29, 29, 31, 30, 26, 26, 27, 26, 25, 28, 27, 25, 25, 25, 25, 24, 25, 23, 20, 15, 20, 1...
$ fl           <chr> "p", "p", "p", "p", "p", "p", "p", "p", "p", "p", "p", "p", "p", "p", "p", "p", "p", ...
$ class        <chr> "compact", "compact", "compact", "compact", "compact", "compact", "compact", "compact...
> |
```

Selecting and filtering data

The `dplyr` package includes special features with regard to selecting and filtering data from the dataset mentioned. We will focus on two functions that will help us to achieve this functionality:

- `select()`
- `filter()`

The select() function

This function is used to choose the required display variables based on specific criteria.

The syntax for calling this function is as follows:

```
select(dataset, column1, column2, ...)
```

The implementation of the `select()` function with respect to our `mpg` dataset is as follows:

```
> mpgSubset <- select(mpg, manufacturer, model) > View(mpgSubset)
```

This subset will only include information relating to the manufacturer and model. We can remove and add our selection criteria as per our requirements:

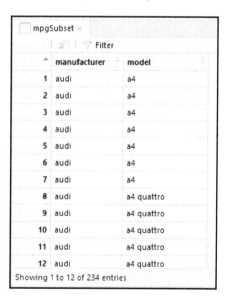

The filter() function

This function helps to keep the observations based on specific criteria. It will filter the dataset records that match the particular condition.

The syntax for implementing the `filter()` function is as follows:

```
filter(data, condition)
```

Here, the parameters refer to the following:

- `data`: The dataset
- `condition`: The condition that is applied for filtering

If we want to filter the records of our dataset whose year of establishment or launch is greater than 2000, it can be achieved with the following syntax:

```
> mpgFilter <- mpg %>%   filter(year>2000)
> View(mpgFilter)
```

The output of our new dataset is as follows:

	manufacturer	model	displ	year	cyl	trans	drv	cty	hwy	fl	class
1	audi	a4	2.0	2008	4	manual(m6)	f	20	31	p	compact
2	audi	a4	2.0	2008	4	auto(av)	f	21	30	p	compact
3	audi	a4	3.1	2008	6	auto(av)	f	18	27	p	compact
4	audi	a4 quattro	2.0	2008	4	manual(m6)	4	20	28	p	compact
5	audi	a4 quattro	2.0	2008	4	auto(s6)	4	19	27	p	compact
6	audi	a4 quattro	3.1	2008	6	auto(s6)	4	17	25	p	compact
7	audi	a4 quattro	3.1	2008	6	manual(m6)	4	15	25	p	compact
8	audi	a6 quattro	3.1	2008	6	auto(s6)	4	17	25	p	midsize
9	audi	a6 quattro	4.2	2008	8	auto(s6)	4	16	23	p	midsize
10	chevrolet	c1500 suburban 2wd	5.3	2008	8	auto(l4)	r	14	20	r	suv
11	chevrolet	c1500 suburban 2wd	5.3	2008	8	auto(l4)	r	11	15	e	suv
12	chevrolet	c1500 suburban 2wd	5.3	2008	8	auto(l4)	r	14	20	r	suv

Showing 1 to 12 of 117 entries

Cleaning and manipulating time series data

In this section, we will focus on cleaning and manipulating time series data of dataset with the help of the `dplyr` package. We will observe the following steps to understand the procedure as a whole:

1. Include the necessary packages in the workspace mentioned:

```
> library(lubridate) # work with dates
Attaching package: 'lubridate'
The following object is masked from 'package:base':
date
> library(dplyr) # data manipulation (filter, summarize, mutate)
> library(ggplot2) # graphics
> library(gridExtra) # tile several plots next to each other
Attaching package: 'gridExtra'
The following object is masked from 'package:dplyr':
combine
> library(scales)
Warning message:
package 'scales' was built under R version 3.5.3
```

2. Now, in order to manipulate time series data, we will consider the main attribute to be the launch year. We need to group the data for our dataset by year:

```
> # Create a group_by object using the year column
> mpg.grp.year <- group_by(mpg, year) # column name to group by
> class(mpg.grp.year)
[1] "grouped_df" "tbl_df" "tbl" "data.frame"
```

3. The `group_by()` function forms a grouped object. This grouped object can then be used to rapidly calculate the summary statistics by group, which, in our case, is the year:

```
> # how many measurements were made each year?
> tally(mpg.grp.year)
# A tibble: 2 x 2
    year       n
<int><int>
1   1999     117
2   2008     117
> summarize(mpg.grp.year,
+           mean(displ)   # calculate the annual mean of displ
+ )
# A tibble: 2 x 2
    year `mean(displ)`
<int><dbl>
```

```
1   1999             3.28
2   2008             3.66
```

4. We can also calculate the mean via the removal of NA values—if there are any—for the displacement (`displ`) attribute:

```
> summarize(mpg.grp.year,
+            mean(displ, na.rm = TRUE)
+ )
# A tibble: 2 x 2
   year `mean(displ, na.rm = TRUE)`
<int><dbl>
1   1999                      3.28
2   2008                      3.66
```

5. Now, it is important to count measurements per year, as mentioned in the following command execution:

```
> mpg %>%
+ group_by(year) %>% # group by year
+ tally() # count measurements per year
# A tibble: 2 x 2
year n
<int><int>
1 1999 117
2 2008 117
```

Piping allows us to perform operations efficiently on our data frame—namely `mpg`—in the following ways:

- Without naming intermediate steps, it allows us to condense our code

- To ensure fast processing, the `dplyr` package is optimized

6. Now, we will consider using the grouping of data with respect to the `year` attribute that is mentioned in the following command:

```
> year.sum <- mpg %>%
+ group_by(year) %>% # group by year
+ summarize(mean(displ, na.rm=TRUE))
> year.sum
# A tibble: 2 x 2
  year `mean(displ, na.rm = TRUE)`
<int><dbl>
1 1999 3.28
2 2008 3.66
```

7. We can now view the structure of the output as follows:

```
> str(year.sum)
Classes 'tbl_df', 'tbl' and 'data.frame':                    2 obs. of  2
variables: $ year                        : int  1999 2008 $
mean(displ, na.rm = TRUE): num  3.28 3.66
```

8. We can plot the attributes grouped in previous steps to represent the time series data representation:

```
> qplot(mpg.grp.year$displ, mpg.grp.year$year,xlab =
"Displacement", ylab = "year",main = "Manipulating Grouped Data")
```

From this, we get the following plot:

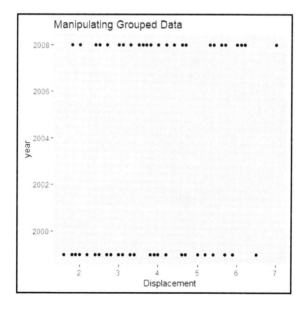

Summary

In this chapter, we listed some of the various packages that are available for reading in various kinds of attributes within the mentioned dataset in R. There are a lot of different options, and even the options we have listed have a wide functionality, which we are going to cover and use as we go further in the book. We learned how to reshape and tidy the erroneous data, along with manipulating and mutating it. By the end of the chapter, we learned how to clean the time series data.

In the next chapter, we will learn to visualize data graphically using the `ggplot2` package. We will also demonstrate how to draw different kinds of plots and charts, such as scatter plots, histograms, probability plots, residual plots, box plots, and block plots.

4
Visualizing Data Graphically with ggplot2

This chapter will demonstrate how to draw different kinds of plots and charts, such as scatter plots, histograms, probability plots, residual plots, box plots, and block plots. We will cover various concepts throughout this chapter, including when we should use different kinds of plots. The code examples in this chapter will utilize the popular R package – ggplot2. We will introduce ggplot2 visualization grammar and learn how to apply it to real-world datasets. We will also demonstrate the examples in this chapter using the `iris` dataset.

The following topics will be covered in this chapter:

- Advanced graphics grammar of ggplot2 for data visualization
- Drawing and customizing scatter plots
- When to use histogram plots and how to draw and customize them
- Visualizing probability plots
- Drawing and customizing residual plots
- Making box plots

Technical requirements

You should have hands-on experience or knowledge of the following points before getting started with this chapter:

- R programming language
- RStudio
- R packages
  (including `readr`, `readxl`, `jsonlite`, `httr`, `rvest`, `DBI`, `dplyr`, `stringr`, `forcats`, `lubridate`, `hms`, `blob`, `ggplot2`, and `knitr`)

Advanced graphics grammar of ggplot2

`ggplot2` is considered one of the primary R packages used for producing statistical or data graphics, and is completely different from other graphics packages. This package functions under grammar called the *grammar of graphics,* which is made up of a set of independent components that can be composed in many ways. *Grammar of graphics* is the only thing that makes `ggplot2` very powerful, because the user is not limited to a set of prespecified graphics that are used in other libraries. The grammar includes a simple set of core principles that render `ggplot2` relatively easy to learn.

In 2005, Wilkinson coined the concept of *grammar of graphics* in order to describe the deep features that underpin all statistical graphics. The concept focuses on the primacy of layers, which includes adapting features embedded with R. So, what does the *grammar of graphics* specify in R? It tells the user that a statistical graphic is used for mapping the data to aesthetic attributes, such as the color, shape, and size of the geometric objects in question, including points, lines, and bars. The plot may also contain various statistical transformations of the data in question that are drawn on the coordinate system being referred to. In addition to this, it includes a feature called *faceting,* which is generally used to create the same plot for different subsets of the dataset mentioned. A particular graphic consists of a combination of these independent components.

Now, let's focus on different types of plots that can be created with reference to the grammar.

Data

Data is used if the user wants to visualize the given set of aesthetic mappings that describe how the requisite variables in the data are mapped together to create mapped aesthetic attributes.

Layers

Layers are made up of geometric elements and the requisite statistical transformations. Layers include **geometric objects** (**geoms**) data, which actually represents the plot with the help of points, lines, polygons, and more. The best demonstration is by binning and counting the observations to create the specific histogram for summarizing the 2D relationship of a specific linear model.

Scales

Scales are used to map values in the data space that is used for the creation of values, be this color, size, or shape. It is worthwhile drawing a legend or axes that are required to provide an inverse mapping, making it possible to read the original data values from the plot specified.

The coordinate system

The coordinate system describes how the data coordinates are mapped together in relation to the specified plane of the graphic. It also provides information on the axes and gridlines, this information being required to read the graph. Normally, this is used as a Cartesian coordinate system, which includes polar coordinates and map projections.

Faceting

Faceting includes specifications on how to break data up into the requisite subsets and how to display the subsets as multiples of data. This is also referred to as a conditioning or latticing process.

Theme

Theme controls the finer points of the display, such as the font size and background color properties. To create an attractive plot, it is always better to consider the built-in options of the theme.

Now, it is also equally important to discuss the limitations or features that grammar doesn't provide:

- It does not suggest which graphics should be used or what the user should do with respect to the plots generated.
- It does not describe the interactivity of data as it includes only a description of static graphics. To create dynamic graphics, alternative solutions should be applied.

As we are now beginning to understand the way in which the ggplot2 package is used, we should now focus on the installation procedure of ggplot2.

Installing ggplot2

Before installing ggplot2, make sure that you have a recent version of R from the official website: http://r-project.org.

Run the following code to install ggplot2:

```
install.packages("ggplot2")
```

From this, we will get the following output:

```
> install.packages("ggplot2")
Installing package into 'C:/Users/Radhika/Documents/R/win-library/3.5'
(as 'lib' is unspecified)
trying URL 'https://cran.rstudio.com/bin/windows/contrib/3.5/ggplot2_3.1.1.zip'
Content type 'application/zip' length 3622219 bytes (3.5 MB)
downloaded 3.5 MB

package 'ggplot2' successfully unpacked and MD5 sums checked

The downloaded binary packages are in
        C:\Users\Radhika\AppData\Local\Temp\RtmpmeKTcs\downloaded_packages
```

Following successful installation, it is important to include the library in the R workspace, as follows:

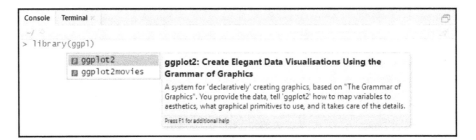

The following output message is generated:

```
> library(ggplot2)

Attaching package: 'ggplot2'

The following object is masked _by_ '.GlobalEnv':

    mpg

Warning message:
package 'ggplot2' was built under R version 3.5.3
> |
```

Now, let's look at scatter plots in the following section.

Scatter plots

In this section, we will be using the `iris` dataset to create the required plots using `ggplot2`.

This dataset includes three Iris species with 50 recorded samples of each, as well as a number of properties relating to each flower, including length, width, and type. One flower species is linearly separable from the other two, but in the other species case, which you can see in the dataset, two are not linearly separable from each other.

The attributes that exist in the dataset are as follows:

- `Id`
- `SepalLengthCm`
- `SepalWidthCm`
- `PetalLengthCm`
- `PetalWidthCm`
- `Species`

In this section, we will focus on creating the scattered plots for the given dataset. Creating scattered plots involves new feature analysis with the help of `ggplot2`. Let's now look at the steps to create scattered plots for our dataset:

1. Include the library in the workspace specified. This involves the execution of the following set of commands:

```
> library('ggplot2')
> library(readr)
```

2. Create the parameters in a systematic way. This will help to resize the plots as desired:

```
> options(repr.plot.width = 6, repr.plot.height = 6)
```

3. This step involves loading the data in our R workspace. The dataset is available at the following link: https://github.com/PacktPublishing/Hands-On-Exploratory-Data-Analysis-with-R/tree/master/ch04. Basically, by means of the following command, we will convert the `.csv` file into a systematic dataset:

```
> Iris <- read.csv('Iris.csv')
> class(Iris)
[1] "data.frame"
```

4. Once the dataset is created, we can view it. This can also be achieved by looking at the first five rows of the dataset:

```
> View(Iris)
> head(Iris)
Id SepalLengthCm SepalWidthCm PetalLengthCm PetalWidthCm Species

1 1 5.1 3.5 1.4 0.2 Iris-setosa
2 2 4.9 3.0 1.4 0.2 Iris-setosa
3 3 4.7 3.2 1.3 0.2 Iris-setosa
4 4 4.6 3.1 1.5 0.2 Iris-setosa
5 5 5.0 3.6 1.4 0.2 Iris-setosa
6 6 5.4 3.9 1.7 0.4 Iris-setosa
```

The `View` function will display the systematic creation of the dataset, which we have achieved successfully by means of the previous set of commands, as shown in the following screenshot:

	Id	SepalLengthCm	SepalWidthCm	PetalLengthCm	PetalWidthCm	Species
1	1	5.1	3.5	1.4	0.2	Iris-setosa
2	2	4.9	3.0	1.4	0.2	Iris-setosa
3	3	4.7	3.2	1.3	0.2	Iris-setosa
4	4	4.6	3.1	1.5	0.2	Iris-setosa
5	5	5.0	3.6	1.4	0.2	Iris-setosa
6	6	5.4	3.9	1.7	0.4	Iris-setosa
7	7	4.6	3.4	1.4	0.3	Iris-setosa
8	8	5.0	3.4	1.5	0.2	Iris-setosa
9	9	4.4	2.9	1.4	0.2	Iris-setosa
10	10	4.9	3.1	1.5	0.1	Iris-setosa
11	11	5.4	3.7	1.5	0.2	Iris-setosa
12	12	4.8	3.4	1.6	0.2	Iris-setosa

Showing 1 to 12 of 150 entries

5. With the help of the `summary()` function, we can also check and analyze the statistical summary of our Iris data:

```
> summary(Iris)
Id SepalLengthCm SepalWidthCm PetalLengthCm PetalWidthCm
Min. : 1.00 Min. :4.300 Min. :2.000 Min. :1.000 Min. :0.100
1st Qu.: 38.25 1st Qu.:5.100 1st Qu.:2.800 1st Qu.:1.600 1st
Qu.:0.300
```

```
Median : 75.50 Median :5.800 Median :3.000 Median :4.350 Median
:1.300
Mean : 75.50 Mean :5.843 Mean :3.054 Mean :3.759 Mean :1.199
3rd Qu.:112.75 3rd Qu.:6.400 3rd Qu.:3.300 3rd Qu.:5.100 3rd
Qu.:1.800
Max. :150.00 Max. :7.900 Max. :4.400 Max. :6.900 Max. :2.500
Species
Iris-setosa :50
Iris-versicolor:50
Iris-virginica :50
```

6. We can then check the relationship between sepal length and sepal width. This can be achieved with the help of a scatter plot creation, which is executed with the help of the following command:

```
> ggplot(data=Iris,aes(x=SepalWidthCm, y=SepalLengthCm)) +
geom_point() + theme_minimal()
```

From this, we get the following plot:

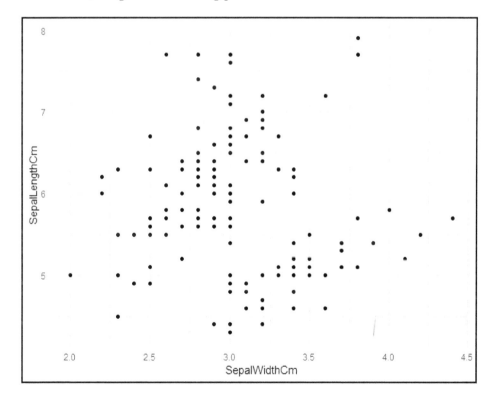

In the preceding `ggplot`, we specify the user data to plot our `iris` datasets. The parameters passed include `x=SepalWidthCm` and `y=SepalLengthCm` to `aes`. In this case, we will get a relationship between the two features, sepal length and sepal width. The simplest way for this to happen is to create a scatter plot, which is achieved with the help of the `geom_point()` function. We can pass an additional aesthetic to our `ggplot`, where species are displayed as legends using different colors:

```
> ggplot(data=Iris,aes(x=SepalWidthCm, y=SepalLengthCm,color=Species)) +
geom_point() + theme_minimal()
```

This gives us the following plot:

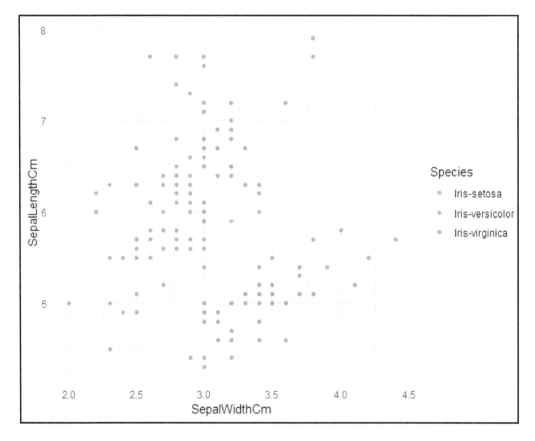

Now, let's look at histogram plots.

Histogram plots

A histogram includes an accurate representation of the distribution of numerical data. It includes a rough estimation of the probability distribution with the continuous variable. It differs from a bar graph. A bar graph compares two variables, and a histogram just one. In this section, we will focus on the use of histogram plots and how to draw and customize them. The `iris` dataset includes fewer attributes, so we can customize them as and when required.

Before understanding the customization of histograms with `ggplot2`, we should understand the normal plotting of the `iris` dataset. The difference between normal plotting and the plots created with `ggplot2` will be clearly visible from the output screenshots.

The following command is executed to create a normal histogram:

```
> hist(iris$Sepal.Width, freq=NULL, density=NULL, breaks=12,
+ xlab="Sepal Width", ylab="Frequency", main="Histogram of Sepal Width")
```

This gives us the following plot:

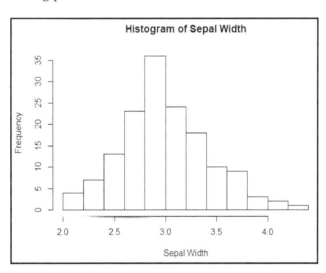

The following steps are observed to create a histogram in a different format:

1. Include the library within the R workspace. This is considered a mandatory step:

    ```
    > library(ggplot2)
    Attaching package: 'ggplot2'
    ```

```
The following object is masked _by_ '.GlobalEnv':
mpg
Warning message:
package 'ggplot2' was built under R version 3.5.3
```

2. Create a histogram with respect to one variable of our dataset, namely `Sepal.Width`:

```
histogram <- ggplot(data=iris, aes(x=Sepal.Width))
```

3. `geom_histogram()` is used for creating histograms with respect to one variable. The output achieved will be more precise and clear in comparison to the normal plots created:

```
histogram + geom_histogram(binwidth=0.2, color="black",
aes(fill=Species)) +
+ xlab("Sepal Width") + ylab("Frequency") + ggtitle("Histogram of
Sepal Width")
```

We then get the following plot:

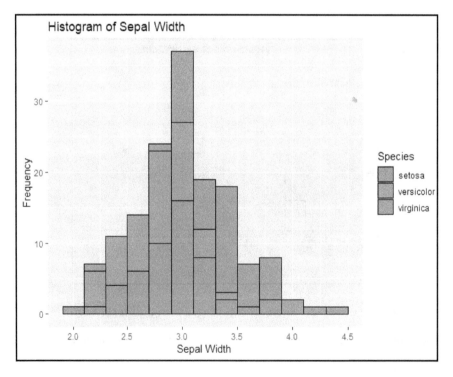

Let's now look at density plots in the next section.

Density plots

The major shortcoming of histograms (which we discussed in an earlier section) is that they are quite sensitive to the choice of bin margins and the number of bins. The best alternative to this is to use density plots, which are regarded as a smoothed version of a histogram. We will implement the following steps to create density plots for an `iris` dataset:

1. Include the library within the R workspace. This is considered a mandatory step:

```
> library(ggplot2)
Attaching package: 'ggplot2'
The following object is masked _by_ '.GlobalEnv':
mpg
Warning message:
package 'ggplot2' was built under R version 3.5.3
```

Ignore the warning messages if there are any. The warning messages are usually determined with respect to system configuration.

2. Have a look at the parameters to determine which plot should be used for density plot creation:

Iris						
	Id	SepalLengthCm	SepalWidthCm	PetalLengthCm	PetalWidthCm	Species
1	1	5.1	3.5	1.4	0.2	Iris-setosa
2	2	4.9	3.0	1.4	0.2	Iris-setosa
3	3	4.7	3.2	1.3	0.2	Iris-setosa
4	4	4.6	3.1	1.5	0.2	Iris-setosa
5	5	5.0	3.6	1.4	0.2	Iris-setosa
6	6	5.4	3.9	1.7	0.4	Iris-setosa
7	7	4.6	3.4	1.4	0.3	Iris-setosa
8	8	5.0	3.4	1.5	0.2	Iris-setosa
9	9	4.4	2.9	1.4	0.2	Iris-setosa
10	10	4.9	3.1	1.5	0.1	Iris-setosa
11	11	5.4	3.7	1.5	0.2	Iris-setosa

Showing 1 to 11 of 150 entries

We will consider taking attributes of `PetalWidthCm` with `Species` in the dataset specified. We have three major species that will be taken into consideration.

3. Implement the density plot with the syntax specified. The difference will be visible from the output that is created:

```
> ggplot(iris) +
+ geom_density(aes(x = Petal.Width, fill = Species), alpha=0.25)
```

The output generated is shown as follows:

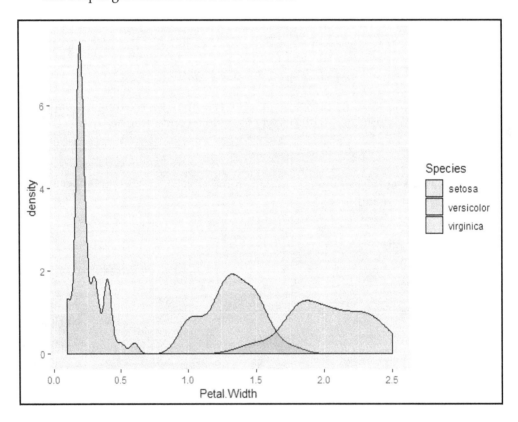

Density plots are considered to be a smoothed version of a histogram. They make some assumptions that affect the visualization with reference to *smoothing bandwidth* (as specified by the bw argument that determines how coarse or granular the density estimation is).

Note that the vertical scale on a density plot will not include longer cuts with respect to frequency. In a density plot, the total area under the plot adds up to one.

Let's now look at probability plots.

Probability plots

This section describes the creation of probability plots in R, which can be used for didactic purposes and predominantly for data analysis purposes. The following functions are available for each distribution of probability plots in the format specified:

Name	Description
dnorm( )	Density or probability function
pnorm( )	Cumulative density function
qnorm( )	Quantile function
Rnorm( )	Random deviates

Let's look at some of the functions mentioned previously.

dnorm()

The first type of plot that will be created based on the density or probability function is named dnorm(). dnorm() will specify the density or the probability for the normal distribution curve. The normal distribution curve, created with the dnorm() function and attribute to be used, for example, PetalWidthCm, can be executed with the following command:

```
> p1 <- ggplot(data = Iris, aes(PetalWidthCm)) +
+ stat_function(fun = dnorm, n = 101, args = list(mean = 0, sd = 1)) +
ylab("") +
+ scale_y_continuous(breaks = NULL)
> p1
```

We get the following plot from this:

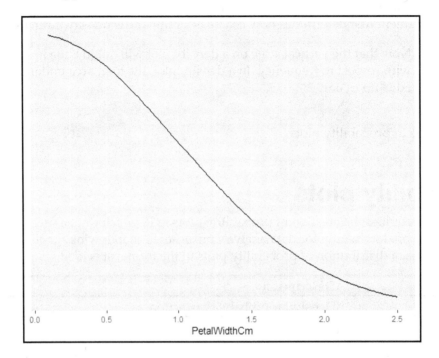

pnorm()

The pnorm() function follows the same constraint, the only difference being that the function generates random numbers with reference to a cumulative density function. We can demonstrate the pnorm() function by executing the following command:

```
> p2 <- ggplot(data = Iris, aes(PetalWidthCm)) +
+ stat_function(fun = pnorm, n = 101, args = list(mean = 0, sd = 1)) +
ylab("") +
+ scale_y_continuous(breaks = NULL)
> p2
```

From this command, we get the following plot:

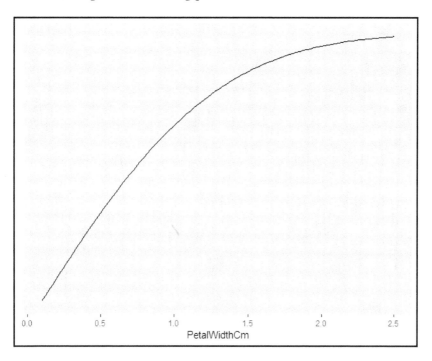

rnorm()

`rnorm()` generates a random value from the normal distribution with the standard syntax specified as follows:

```
rnorm(n, mean = , sd = )
```

This is used to generate n number of normal random numbers with the argument's mean and sd. For our dataset, we can execute the following command to observe the probability curve:

```
> p4 <- ggplot(data = Iris, aes(PetalWidthCm)) +
+ stat_function(fun = rnorm, n = 101, args = list(mean = 0, sd = 1)) +
ylab("") +
+ scale_y_continuous(breaks = NULL)
> p4
```

From this, we get the following plot:

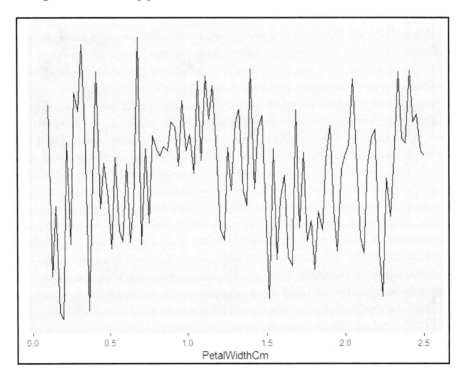

Let's now look at box plots.

Box plots

Box plots include a simple way of representing statistical data of the given plot in which the rectangle is drawn, including the second and third quartiles. The vertical line is used to indicate the median value, while the lower and upper quartiles are displayed on either side of the rectangle. We can create and customize the box plot using the steps mentioned as follows:

1. Include the library within the R workspace. This is considered a mandatory step:

```
> library(ggplot2)
Attaching package: 'ggplot2'
The following object is masked _by_ '.GlobalEnv':
mpg
Warning message:
package 'ggplot2' was built under R version 3.5.3
```

2. Use the required function, such as we did for scattered plots, to get the perpendicular plots arranged in a systematic manner:

```
> ggplot(data=Iris,aes(x=Species, y=SepalLengthCm,color=Species)) +
geom_boxplot() +theme_minimal()+
+ theme(legend.position="none")
```

We get the following plot from this:

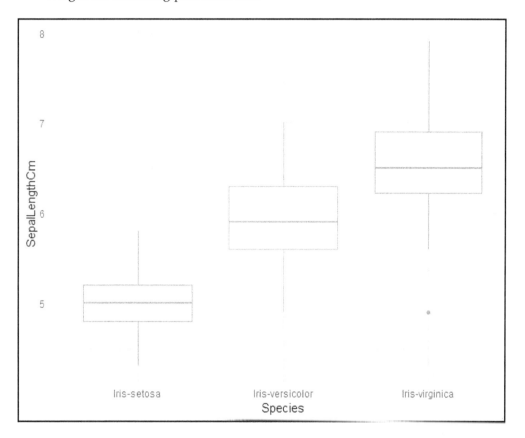

3. The variation of the box plot can be created with another function called geom_violin, which represents the violin structure of the box plots:

```
> ggplot(data=Iris,aes(x=Species, y=SepalLengthCm,color=Species)) +
geom_violin() +theme_minimal()+
+ theme(legend.position="none")
```

Here, we get the following plot:

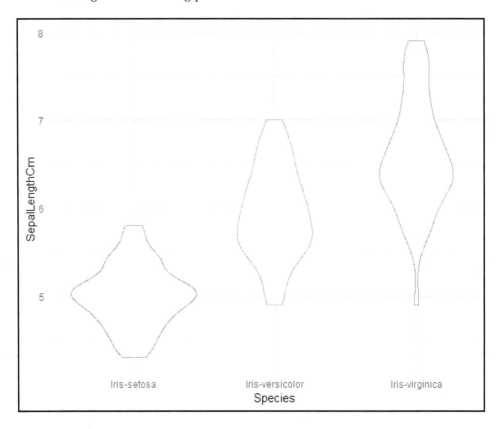

Residual plots

A residual plot is a graph that displays the residuals on the vertical axis specified and the independent variable on the horizontal axis. In the event that the points in a residual plot are dispersed in a random manner around the horizontal axis, it is appropriate to use a linear regression model for the data. If the data is not dispersed, a non-linear model is more appropriate.

We can create and customize the residual plot using the steps mentioned as follows:

1. Include the library within the R workspace. This is considered a mandatory step:

    ```
    > library(ggplot2)
    Attaching package: 'ggplot2'
    The following object is masked _by_ '.GlobalEnv':
    mpg
    Warning message:
    package 'ggplot2' was built under R version 3.5.3
    ```

2. Use the required function, such as we did for scatter plots, to get the perpendicular plots arranged in a systematic manner:

    ```
    > ggplot(lm(Sepal.Length~Sepal.Width, data=iris)) +
    geom_point(aes(x=.fitted, y=.resid))
    ```

    We get the following residual plot as a result:

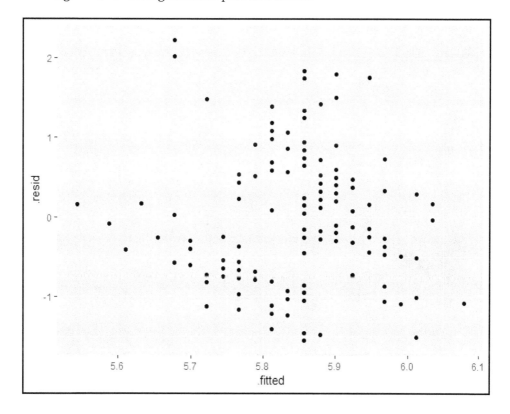

Summary

In this chapter, we have focused on the implementation of the `ggplot2()` library, which is considered to be a data visualization library. We have listed some of the various packages that are available for reading various kinds of attributes within the mentioned dataset in R. Many different options are available, and even the options we have listed have a wide functionality, which we are going to cover and use as we go further into the book. In this chapter, we mainly covered different plots, including scatter plots, histogram plots, density plots, probability plots, and box plots.

In the next chapter, we will learn how to use RStudio to wrap your code, graphics, plots, and findings in a complete and informative data analysis report, and how to publish it in different formats for different audiences using R markdown and packages such as `knitr`.

5
Creating Aesthetically Pleasing Reports with knitr and R Markdown

In this chapter, we will learn how to use RStudio to wrap your code, graphics, plots, and findings (such as the representation of reports of the data frame) in a complete and informative data analysis report. We will also learn how to publish it in different formats for different audiences using R Markdown and packages such as `knitr`. Finally, we will learn how to customize data reports and export data in different formats.

The following topics will be covered in this chapter:

- Learning R Markdown concepts
- Producing reproducible data analysis reports with `knitr`
- Customizing your data reports
- Exporting in different formats

Technical requirements

You should have hands-on experience or knowledge of the following points before getting started with this chapter:

- R programming language
- RStudio
- R packages
  (including `readr`, `readxl`, `jsonlite`, `httr`, `rvest`, `DBI`, `dplyr`, `stringr`, `forcats`, `lubridate`, `hms`, `blob`, `ggplot2`, and `knitr`)

Installing R Markdown

R Markdown is known for providing an authoring framework for data science. R Markdown can be used for the following functionality:

- Executing and saving code
- Generating high-quality reports that can be shared with an audience

R Markdown was designed for easy reproducibility with respect to the computing code, and narratives with respect to the code and output that is generated. The results are generated with the respective source code. R Markdown supports a lot of static, dynamic, and interactive output formats. Let's now focus on the installation procedure of R Markdown.

As discussed in the previous chapters, it is assumed that you have already installed RStudio IDE. This IDE is not required but is usually recommended, as it makes it easier for a developer to work with R Markdown.

Please follow these steps to install the rmarkdown package in R:

1. To install the rmarkdown package in R, the following command is executed:

```
> install.packages("rmarkdown")
```

We get the following output:

```
> install.packages("rmarkdown")
Installing package into 'C:/Users/Radhika/Documents/R/win-library/3.5'
(as 'lib' is unspecified)
also installing the dependencies 'evaluate', 'tinytex'

trying URL 'https://cran.rstudio.com/bin/windows/contrib/3.5/evaluate_0.13.zip'
Content type 'application/zip' length 73984 bytes (72 KB)
downloaded 72 KB

trying URL 'https://cran.rstudio.com/bin/windows/contrib/3.5/tinytex_0.12.zip'
Content type 'application/zip' length 95068 bytes (92 KB)
downloaded 92 KB

trying URL 'https://cran.rstudio.com/bin/windows/contrib/3.5/rmarkdown_1.12.zip'
Content type 'application/zip' length 3564083 bytes (3.4 MB)
downloaded 3.4 MB

package 'evaluate' successfully unpacked and MD5 sums checked
package 'tinytex' successfully unpacked and MD5 sums checked
package 'rmarkdown' successfully unpacked and MD5 sums checked

The downloaded binary packages are in
        C:\Users\Radhika\AppData\Local\Temp\RtmpWQm2mB\downloaded_packages
```

2. `tinytex` is defined as a lightweight, portable, cross-platform LaTeX distribution with easy maintenance. The R `tinytex` companion package can help the user automatically install missing LaTeX packages when LaTeX files, or R Markdown documents, are converted to PDF. It also ensures that a LaTeX document is compiled for the correct number of times to resolve all the cross-reference issues. The installation can be achieved through the following command:

```
> install.packages("tinytex")
```

We get the following output:

```
> install.packages("tinytex")
Installing package into 'C:/Users/Radhika/Documents/R/win-library/3.5'
(as 'lib' is unspecified)
trying URL 'https://cran.rstudio.com/bin/windows/contrib/3.5/tinytex_0.12.zip'
Content type 'application/zip' length 94822 bytes (92 KB)
downloaded 92 KB

package 'tinytex' successfully unpacked and MD5 sums checked

The downloaded binary packages are in
        C:\Users\Radhika\AppData\Local\Temp\RtmpwQm2mB\downloaded_packages
>
```

3. The `knitr` package is designed to create a transparent engine for dynamic report generation with R. The installation procedure also requires the execution of the following command. As we will focus on report generation in the *Reproducible data analysis reports with knitr* section of this chapter, we need this package for further development:

```
> install.packages("knitr")
```

We get the following output:

```
> install.packages("knitr")
Installing package into 'C:/Users/Radhika/Documents/R/win-library/3.5'
(as 'lib' is unspecified)
also installing the dependency 'xfun'

trying URL 'https://cran.rstudio.com/bin/windows/contrib/3.5/xfun_0.6.zip'
Content type 'application/zip' length 166880 bytes (162 KB)
downloaded 162 KB

trying URL 'https://cran.rstudio.com/bin/windows/contrib/3.5/knitr_1.22.zip'
Content type 'application/zip' length 1470245 bytes (1.4 MB)
downloaded 1.4 MB

package 'xfun' successfully unpacked and MD5 sums checked
package 'knitr' successfully unpacked and MD5 sums checked

The downloaded binary packages are in
        C:\Users\Radhika\AppData\Local\Temp\RtmpwQm2mB\downloaded_packages
> |
```

Working with R Markdown

The following steps are used to start with R Markdown:

1. Open RStudio IDE
2. Install the respective packages needed
3. Create a new R Markdown document as follows: select the **Menu** option by navigating to **File | New File | R Markdown**
4. The following screenshot shows the lookup of the required Markdown page:

```
---
title: "Introduction"
output: html_document
---

```{r setup, include=FALSE}
knitr::opts_chunk$set(echo = TRUE)
```

R Markdown

This is an R Markdown document. Markdown is a simple formatting syntax for
authoring HTML, PDF, and MS Word documents. For more details on using R
Markdown see <http://rmarkdown.rstudio.com>.

When you click the **Knit** button a document will be generated that includes
both content as well as the output of any embedded R code chunks within the
document. You can embed an R code chunk like this:

```{r cars}
```

```
Introduction ⬍                                              R Markdown ⬍

The attributes shown in the preceding screenshot are as follows:

- **Title**: Holds the title name
- **Output**: The kind of output needed

This is the sample R Markdown document that can be used for further authoring of HTML, PDF, and the respective MS Word documents.

# Reproducible data analysis reports with knitr

As discussed in the previous section, `knitr` is used to design pleasing reports in R. R Markdown provides a simple syntax to define analysis reports. Based on the definitions of report generation, `knitr` can generate reports in various formats such as HTML, PDF, Microsoft Word, and several presentation formats. R Markdown documents usually contain regular text, embedded R code chunks, and inline R code. A `knitr` package parses the Markdown document with the insertion of results for executing the R code, at mentioned locations within the regular text, to create a well-formatted report. This refers to the breakdown of statements of R to create a report that is easy to understand.

We will use the following dataset for creating aesthetically pleasing reports with `knitr` and RStudio.

The data includes technical specs of automobiles, specifically cars. The download link is as follows: `https://github.com/PacktPublishing/Hands-On-Exploratory-Data-Analysis-with-R/tree/master/ch05`.

For more information on the dataset, you can refer to the following link: `https://archive.ics.uci.edu/ml/machine-learning-databases/auto-mpg/`.

For creating reproducible reports, we will use the following steps:

1. Import the dataset from the URL in the R workspace.

```
> library(readr)
> Autompg <- read.csv("auto-mpg.csv")
> Autompg
> View(Autompg)
```

The dataset is as follows:

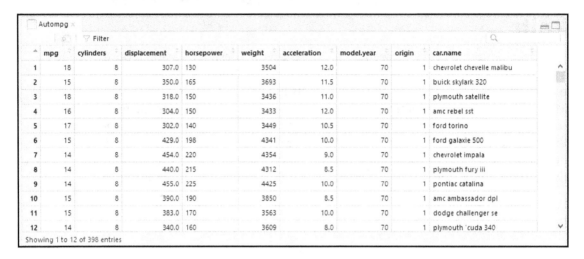

	mpg	cylinders	displacement	horsepower	weight	acceleration	model.year	origin	car.name
1	18	8	307.0	130	3504	12.0	70	1	chevrolet chevelle malibu
2	15	8	350.0	165	3693	11.5	70	1	buick skylark 320
3	18	8	318.0	150	3436	11.0	70	1	plymouth satellite
4	16	8	304.0	150	3433	12.0	70	1	amc rebel sst
5	17	8	302.0	140	3449	10.5	70	1	ford torino
6	15	8	429.0	198	4341	10.0	70	1	ford galaxie 500
7	14	8	454.0	220	4354	9.0	70	1	chevrolet impala
8	14	8	440.0	215	4312	8.5	70	1	plymouth fury iii
9	14	8	455.0	225	4425	10.0	70	1	pontiac catalina
10	15	8	390.0	190	3850	8.5	70	1	amc ambassador dpl
11	15	8	383.0	170	3563	10.0	70	1	dodge challenger se
12	14	8	340.0	160	3609	8.0	70	1	plymouth 'cuda 340

Showing 1 to 12 of 398 entries

2. Create a new R Markdown document as follows: select the **Menu** option by navigating to **File** | **New File** | **R Markdown**:

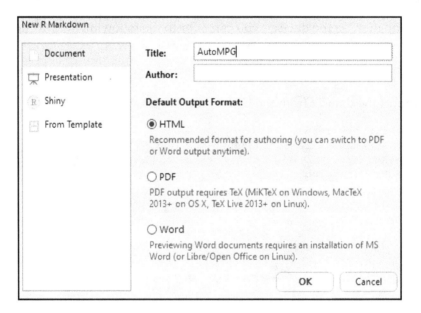

The default output formats include HTML, PDF, and Word formats. Here, we will focus on creating a report in HTML format from the dataset.

3. Once the new Markdown document is created, you can see the output in the following screenshot:

```
AutoMPG.Rmd
                        Knit                                              Insert         Run
1    ---
2    title: "AutoMPG"
3    output: html_document
4    author: Radhika
5    ---
6
7    ```{r setup, include=FALSE}
8    knitr::opts_chunk$set(echo = TRUE)
9    ```
10
11   ## R Markdown
12
13   This is an R Markdown document. Markdown is a simple formatting syntax for authoring HTML, PDF, and
     MS word documents. For more details on using R Markdown see <http://rmarkdown.rstudio.com>.
14
15   when you click the **Knit** button a document will be generated that includes both content as well as
     the output of any embedded R code chunks within the document. You can embed an R code chunk like
     this:
16
17   ```{r cars}
18   summary(cars)
19   ```
20
21   ## Including Plots
22
23   You can also embed plots, for example:
24
25   ```{r pressure, echo=FALSE}
26   plot(pressure)
```

The main attributes that were defined in the document creation are mentioned in the beginning. This includes the **title**, **output**, and **author** attributes with specific values. For our convenience, the file is saved as `AutoMPG.Rmd`. The `.Rmd` extension refers to the R Markdown files.

4. If we wish to have a look at the summary of the dataset that we had imported in our initial steps, that is, `AutoMPG`, it can be done by executing the following command, which includes the required functions within R Markdown:

```
```{Summary of dataset imported}
summary(Autompg)
```

Including Plots
You can also embed plots, for example:
```{r pressure, echo=FALSE}
plot(Autompg$mpg~Autompg$weight)
```
```

You can run the R Markdown document, as shown in the following screenshot, and the output will be generated as per the function calls:

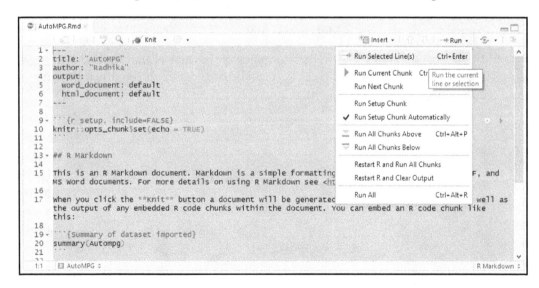

To create a report of a selected line, we need to follow these steps:

The summary information is generated, as shown in the following code block:

```
> summary(Autompg)
 mpg cylinders displacement horsepower weight acceleration
 Min.  : 9.00 Min. :3.000 Min. : 68.0 150 : 22 Min. :1613 Min.  :
8.00
 1st Qu.:17.50 1st Qu.:4.000 1st Qu.:104.2 90 : 20 1st Qu.:2224 1st
Qu.:13.82
 Median :23.00 Median :4.000 Median :148.5 88 : 19 Median :2804
Median :15.50
 Mean :23.51 Mean :5.455 Mean :193.4 110 : 18 Mean :2970 Mean
:15.57
 3rd Qu.:29.00 3rd Qu.:8.000 3rd Qu.:262.0 100 : 17 3rd Qu.:3608
3rd Qu.:17.18
 Max. :46.60 Max. :8.000 Max. :455.0 75 : 14 Max. :5140 Max. :24.80
 (Other):288
 model.year origin car.name
 Min. :70.00 Min. :1.000 ford pinto : 6
 1st Qu.:73.00 1st Qu.:1.000 amc matador : 5
 Median :76.00 Median :1.000 ford maverick : 5
 Mean :76.01 Mean :1.573 toyota corolla: 5
 3rd Qu.:79.00 3rd Qu.:2.000 amc gremlin : 4
 Max. :82.00 Max. :3.000 amc hornet : 4
 (Other) :369
```

The following screenshot shows a scatter plot that describes the variability of the mpg and weight attributes:

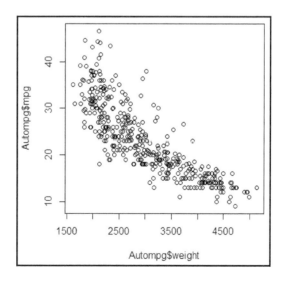

Exporting and customizing reports

We will now focus on customizing the reports with export functionality in the required format. The best illustration of the export format can be considered using the PDF format. We will carry out the following steps to create the export in PDF format:

1. Create a Markdown document with a default output format in PDF, as shown in the following screenshot:

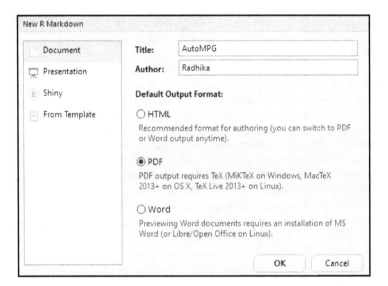

2. The Markdown is created with the required attributes of **title**, **author**, the **output** format, and the **date** format, as follows:

```
---
title: "AutoMPG"
author: "Radhika"
date: "May 7, 2019"
output: pdf_document
---

```{r setup, include=FALSE}
knitr::opts_chunk$set(echo = TRUE)
```

R Markdown

This is an R Markdown document. Markdown is a simple formatting syntax for
authoring HTML, PDF, and MS Word documents. For more details on using R Markdown
see <http://rmarkdown.rstudio.com>.

When you click the **Knit** button a document will be generated that includes both
content as well as the output of any embedded R code chunks within the document.
You can embed an R code chunk like this:
```

3. We can implement the same functions that were used in the previous example, while creating the required HTML documents, that is, fetching the summary of data and plotting the attributes, which is considered as a scatter plot:

```
> summary(Autompg)
 mpg cylinders displacement horsepower weight acceleration
 Min. : 9.00 Min. :3.000 Min. : 68.0 150 : 22 Min. :1613 Min. :
8.00
 1st Qu.:17.50 1st Qu.:4.000 1st Qu.:104.2 90 : 20 1st Qu.:2224 1st
Qu.:13.82
 Median :23.00 Median :4.000 Median :148.5 88 : 19 Median :2804
Median :15.50
 Mean :23.51 Mean :5.455 Mean :193.4 110 : 18 Mean :2970 Mean
:15.57
 3rd Qu.:29.00 3rd Qu.:8.000 3rd Qu.:262.0 100 : 17 3rd Qu.:3608
3rd Qu.:17.18
 Max. :46.60 Max. :8.000 Max. :455.0 75 : 14 Max. :5140 Max. :24.80
 (Other):288
model.year origin car.name
 Min. :70.00 Min. :1.000 ford pinto : 6
 1st Qu.:73.00 1st Qu.:1.000 amc matador : 5
 Median :76.00 Median :1.000 ford maverick : 5
 Mean :76.01 Mean :1.573 toyota corolla: 5
 3rd Qu.:79.00 3rd Qu.:2.000 amc gremlin : 4
 Max. :82.00 Max. :3.000 amc hornet : 4
 (Other) :369
```

The following screenshot shows the scatter plot:

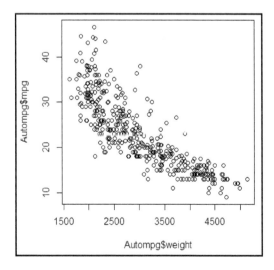

4. With the export feature using `knitr`, we can convert the output to the required format. We need it in PDF format as follows:

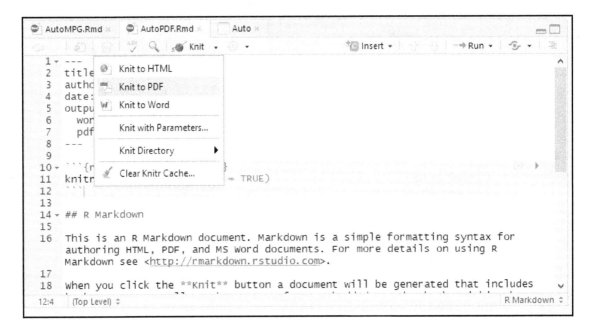

The PDF format is created in the local directory that is represented as follows:

Name	Date modified	Type	Size
AutoPDF.Rmd	5/8/2019 2:16 PM	RMD File	1 KB
AutoPDF	5/8/2019 2:08 PM	Adobe Acrobat D...	1 KB
AutoMPG.Rmd	5/8/2019 2:05 PM	RMD File	1 KB
auto-mpg	5/8/2019 10:28 AM	Microsoft Excel C...	18 KB

Summary

In this chapter, we focused on the implementation of the R Markdown feature, which is considered important from a report-generation point of view. We have listed some of the various packages that are available for reading in various kinds of attributes, within the mentioned dataset in R. There are lot of different options, and even the options we have listed have a wide functionality that we are going to cover and use as we go further through the book.

In the next chapter, we will take a real-world univariate and control dataset and run a complete exploratory data analysis workflow on it using the R packages and techniques we have already covered.

Section 2: Univariate, Time Series, and Multivariate Data

2

In this section, we will learn about the complete process of exploratory data analysis in R using real-world datasets from different problem areas, involving univariate and control datasets, as well as time series and multivariate data.

The following chapters will be covered in this section:

Chapter 6, *Univariate and Control Datasets*

Chapter 7, *Time Series Datasets*

Chapter 8, *Multivariate Datasets*

6
Univariate and Control Datasets

In this chapter, we will take a real-world univariate and control dataset and run a complete exploratory data analysis workflow on it using the R packages and techniques we covered in `Chapter 1`, *Setting Up Our Data Analysis Environment*. After reading and tidying up the data, we will use EDA techniques to map and understand the underlying structure of the data. We will then identify the most important variables in the dataset, test our assumptions to estimate the parameters, and establish the margins of error. We will then explore the dataset graphically using four plots and probability plots. And finally, we will summarize our results in a data report. The code examples will be used from the *Bank and Marketing data* from UCI.

The following topics will be covered in this chapter:

- Introducing and reading the data
- Cleaning and tidying up the data
- Mapping and understanding the underlying structure of the dataset
- Identifying the most important variables in your dataset
- Checking assumptions with model fit criteria or a hypothesis test
- Creating a list of outliers or other anomalies using the Tietjen-Moore test
- Uncovering a parsimonious model
- Estimating parameters and establishing the margins of error
- Calculating the correlation coefficient
- Exploring the data graphically by means of probability plots
- Summarizing our findings

Technical requirements

You should have hands-on experience or knowledge of the following points before getting started with this chapter:

- R programming language
- RStudio
- R packages
  (including `readr`, `readxl`, `jsonlite`, `httr`, `rvest`, `DBI`, `dplyr`, `stringr`, `forc ats`, `lubridate`, `hms`, `blob`, `ggplot2`, and `knitr`)

Reading the dataset

In this chapter, we will focus on a dataset that includes classic marketing data from a bank dataset that is available on the UCI Machine Learning Repository. This dataset includes complete information regarding a marketing campaign undertaken by a financial institution that assists in analyzing future strategies with a view to improving future marketing campaigns for the bank. We can access the dataset using the following link:

```
https://github.com/PacktPublishing/Hands-On-Exploratory-Data-Analysis-with-R/
tree/master/ch06
```

For more information on the dataset, you can access the following link:

```
https://archive.ics.uci.edu/ml/datasets/bank+marketing
```

Now, we will introduce this dataset within the R workspace for further manipulation and implementation. The following steps are required to introduce and read the dataset:

1. Include the requisite libraries for converting the CSV file to the required dataset within the R workspace:

   ```
   > library(readr)
   Warning message:
   package 'arules' was built under R version 3.5.1
   > bank <-read.csv("bank.csv", stringsAsFactors = FALSE)
   > bank
   ```

2. We can view the data using the `View()` function, shown as follows:

```
> View(bank)
```

This gives us the following output:

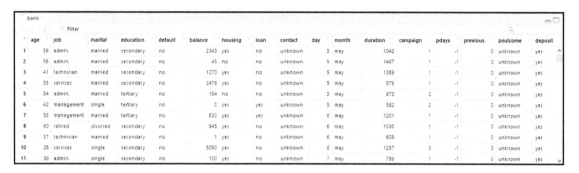

The important attributes that we will implement in the later sections of code implementation are as follows:

- `age`
- `job`
- `marital` (marital status)
- `education`
- `default`
- `balance`
- `housing`
- `loan`
- `contact`
- `day`
- `month`
- `duration`
- `pdays` (refers to the number of days that have elapsed since the customer was last contacted)
- `previous`
- `poutcome` (refers to the outcome of the previous campaign)
- `deposit`

Let's now proceed with cleaning and tidying up the data.

Cleaning and tidying up the data

Data cleaning, or rather tidying up the data, is the process of transforming the raw data into a specific form of consistent data that includes a simpler form of analysis. Cleaning the attributes of the bank dataset is considered quite critical and should be performed carefully. The R workspace includes a set of comprehensive tools that are specifically designed to clean the data in an effective manner. The following steps are implemented to this end:

1. Initial explanatory analysis
2. Data visualization
3. Error cleaning

Here, we will focus on various aspects of understanding the data summary and also getting a feel for the data. We will also implement the libraries required to clean and tidy up the data by observing the following steps:

1. Include the requisite libraries (as discussed in Chapter 3, *Examining, Cleaning, and Filtering*) that assist in cleaning and tidying up the data:

```
> library(tidyr)
Attaching package: 'tidyr'
The following object is masked _by_ '.GlobalEnv':
who
The following object is masked from 'package:Matrix':
expand
Warning message:
package 'tidyr' was built under R version 3.5.3

> library(dplyr)
Attaching package: 'dplyr'
The following objects are masked from 'package:arules':
intersect, recode, setdiff, setequal, union
The following objects are masked from 'package:stats':
filter, lag
The following objects are masked from 'package:base':
intersect, setdiff, setequal, union
Warning message:
package 'dplyr' was built under R version 3.5.3
```

2. Getting a feel for the data is achieved by executing the following command:

```
> class(bank)
[1] "data.frame"

> dim(bank)
[1] 11162 17
```

3. View the column names of the required dataset:

```
> colnames(bank)

[1] "age" "job" "marital" "education" "default" "balance" "housing"
[8] "loan" "contact" "day" "month" "duration" "campaign" "pdays"
[15] "previous" "poutcome" "deposit"
```

4. View the structure of the data:

```
>
str(bank)
'data.frame': 11162 obs. of 17 variables:
$ age : int 59 56 41 55 54 42 56 60 37 28 ...
$ job : chr "admin." "admin." "technician" "services" ...
$ marital : chr "married" "married" "married" "married" ...
$ education: chr "secondary" "secondary" "secondary" "secondary"
...
$ default : chr "no" "no" "no" "no" ...
$ balance : int 2343 45 1270 2476 184 0 830 545 1 5090 ...
$ housing : chr "yes" "no" "yes" "yes" ...
$ loan : chr "no" "no" "no" "no" ...
$ contact : chr "unknown" "unknown" "unknown" "unknown" ...
$ day : int 5 5 5 5 5 5 6 6 6 6 ...
$ month : chr "may" "may" "may" "may" ...
$ duration : int 1042 1467 1389 579 673 562 1201 1030 608 1297 ...
$ campaign : int 1 1 1 1 2 2 1 1 1 3 ...
$ pdays : int -1 -1 -1 -1 -1 -1 -1 -1 -1 -1 ...
$ previous : int 0 0 0 0 0 0 0 0 0 0 ...
$ poutcome : chr "unknown" "unknown" "unknown" "unknown" ...
$ deposit : chr "yes" "yes" "yes" "yes" ...
```

5. Now, let's analyze the structure and summary of the data, which will help us to focus on cleaning and tidying it up:

```
> summary(bank)

age job marital education default

Min. :18.00 Length:11162 Length:11162 Length:11162 Length:11162
```

1st Qu.:32.00 Class :character Class :character Class :character Class :character

Median :39.00 Mode :character Mode :character Mode :character Mode :character

Mean :41.23

3rd Qu.:49.00

Max. :95.00

balance housing loan contact day

Min. :-6847 Length:11162 Length:11162 Length:11162 Min. : 1.00

1st Qu.: 122 Class :character Class :character Class :character 1st Qu.: 8.00

Median : 550 Mode :character Mode :character Mode :character Median :15.00

Mean : 1529 Mean :15.66

3rd Qu.: 1708 3rd Qu.:22.00

Max. :81204
Max. :31.00

month duration campaign pdays previous

Length:11162 Min. : 2 Min. : 1.000 Min. : -1.00 Min. : 0.0000

Class :character 1st Qu.: 138 1st Qu.: 1.000 1st Qu.: -1.00 1st Qu.: 0.0000

Mode :character Median : 255 Median : 2.000 Median : -1.00 Median : 0.0000

Mean : 372 Mean : 2.508 Mean : 51.33 Mean : 0.8326

3rd Qu.: 496 3rd Qu.: 3.000 3rd Qu.: 20.75 3rd Qu.: 1.0000

Max. :3881 Max. :63.000 Max. :854.00 Max. :58.0000

poutcome deposit

Length:11162 Length:11162

```
Class :character Class :character

Mode :character Mode :character
```

6. It is important to visualize the data in different patterns. The histogram can be used to analyze the numeric columns. In order to plot the histogram for a specific column, the following code needs to be executed:

```
> library(plyr)

> hist(bank$balance)
```

This gives us the following plot:

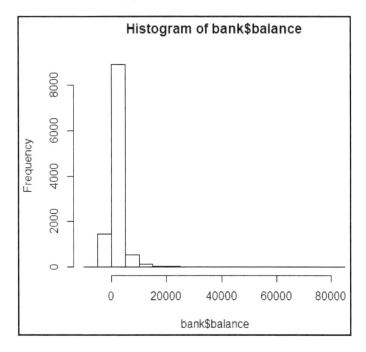

7. Here, we will analyze the `balance` column, which provides a range from **0** to **20000**, which means that the data is concentrated toward a particular value. This can also be framed with a `boxplot` by executing the following command:

```
> boxplot(bank$balance)
```

This gives us the following plot:

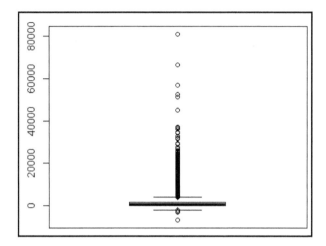

8. This step involves correcting the errors. At times, an incorrect type is associated with these columns. Columns containing the text elements are stored as numeric columns. When this happens, the data type needs to be changed using the following code:

```
> class(bank$balance)

[1] "integer"

> bank$balance<-as.character(bank$balance)

> class(bank$balance)

[1] "character"
```

String manipulation in R is useful when someone is working with datasets containing a plethora of text elements. We will be focusing on two attributes, namely, balance and loan, which helps us to analyze whether the customer is eligible for a loan based on the parameters indicated.

9. We will combine two columns in our data frame to get the loan parameters, as specified in the following code:

```
> library(tidyr)

> bank1<-unite(data = bank, col= balance, loan)

> bank1
```

This gives us the following output:

	age	job	marital	education	default	housing	contact	balance	day	month	duration	
6	42	management	single	tertiary	no	yes	unknown	yes	5	may	562	^
7	56	management	married	tertiary	no	yes	unknown	yes	6	may	1201	
13	29	management	married	tertiary	no	yes	unknown	yes	7	may	1689	
20	49	admin.	divorced	secondary	no	yes	unknown	yes	8	may	513	
41	60	blue-collar	married	primary	no	yes	unknown	yes	13	may	1015	
52	39	management	divorced	tertiary	no	yes	unknown	yes	14	may	1328	
53	59	retired	married	secondary	no	yes	unknown	yes	14	may	1125	
67	49	unknown	married	primary	no	yes	unknown	yes	15	may	520	
77	39	technician	married	tertiary	no	yes	unknown	yes	16	may	813	
81	29	admin.	single	secondary	no	yes	unknown	yes	16	may	803	v

We will now compare the two datasets, namely, `bank1` and `bank`, to obtain the output in a desirable format.

Understanding the structure of the data

Now, let's understand the underlying structure of the data using the following steps. This may involve certain type conversions, which are mentioned as follows:

1. Check the summary of the dataset created:

```
> summary(bank)

 age job marital education default

 Min. :18.00 Length:11162 Length:11162 Length:11162 Length:11162

 1st Qu.:32.00 Class :character Class :character Class :character Class :character

 Median :39.00 Mode :character Mode :character Mode :character Mode :character

 Mean :41.23

 3rd Qu.:49.00

 Max. :95.00
```

```
balance housing loan contact day

Length:11162 Length:11162 Length:11162 Length:11162 Min.  : 1.00

Class :character Class :character Class :character Class
:character 1st Qu.: 8.00

Mode :character Mode :character Mode :character Mode :character
Median :15.00

Mean :15.66

3rd Qu.:22.00

Max.  :31.00

month duration campaign pdays previous

Length:11162 Min.  : 2 Min.  : 1.000 Min.  : -1.00 Min.  : 0.0000

Class :character 1st Qu.: 138 1st Qu.: 1.000 1st Qu.: -1.00 1st
Qu.: 0.0000

Mode :character Median : 255 Median : 2.000 Median : -1.00 Median
: 0.0000

Mean : 372 Mean : 2.508 Mean : 51.33 Mean : 0.8326

3rd Qu.: 496 3rd Qu.: 3.000 3rd Qu.: 20.75 3rd Qu.: 1.0000

Max.  :3881 Max.  :63.000 Max.  :854.00 Max.  :58.0000

poutcome deposit

Length:11162 Length:11162

Class :character Class :character

Mode :character Mode :character
```

It represents five quartiles:

- The first quartile (25%) is a quarter of the way along from the first observation to the last observation
- The median is the middle value of the observation that divides the data into two halves
- The mean is the average value

- The third quartile (75%) is three quarters of the way along from the first observation to the last observation
- `Max` represents the maximum value

2. Create the type conversions as per the attribute name, which will help in hypothesis test creation—the primary focus of our next section:

```
> bank$age<-as.numeric(bank$age)
> bank$job<-as.character(bank$job)
> bank$marital<-as.character(bank$marital)
> bank$education<-as.character(bank$education)
> bank$default<-as.character(bank$default)
> bank$balance<-as.numeric(bank$balance)
> bank$housing<-as.character(bank$loan)
> bank$contact<- as.character(bank$contact)
> bank$day<-as.numeric(bank$day)
> bank$month<-as.character(bank$month)
> bank$duration<-as.numeric(bank$duration)
> bank$campaign<-as.numeric(bank$campaign)
```

The dataset is visible using the `View()` function, as follows:

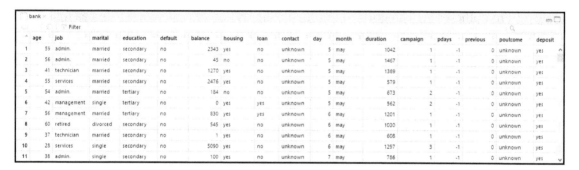

	age	job	marital	education	default	balance	housing	loan	contact	day	month	duration	campaign	pdays	previous	poutcome	deposit
1	59	admin.	married	secondary	no	2343	yes	no	unknown	5	may	1042	1	-1	0	unknown	yes
2	56	admin.	married	secondary	no	45	no	no	unknown	5	may	1467	1	-1	0	unknown	yes
3	41	technician	married	secondary	no	1270	yes	no	unknown	5	may	1389	1	-1	0	unknown	yes
4	55	services	married	secondary	no	2476	yes	no	unknown	5	may	579	1	-1	0	unknown	yes
5	54	admin.	married	tertiary	no	184	no	no	unknown	5	may	673	2	-1	0	unknown	yes
6	42	management	single	tertiary	no	0	yes	yes	unknown	5	may	562	2	-1	0	unknown	yes
7	56	management	married	tertiary	no	830	yes	yes	unknown	6	may	1201	1	-1	0	unknown	yes
8	60	retired	divorced	secondary	no	545	yes	no	unknown	6	may	1030	1	-1	0	unknown	yes
9	37	technician	married	secondary	no	1	yes	no	unknown	6	may	608	1	-1	0	unknown	yes
10	28	services	single	secondary	no	5090	yes	no	unknown	6	may	1297	3	-1	0	unknown	yes
11	38	admin.	single	secondary	no	100	yes	no	unknown	7	may	786	1	-1	0	unknown	yes

The important attributes to work on here are the following:

- `age`
- `balance`
- `housing`
- `loan`
- `month`
- `deposit`
- `duration`

These parameters will help us to get the loan parameters, such as the age group of the list of customers from the dataset for the loan specified.

Hypothesis tests

The hypothesis test in R is an assumption made by the researcher to examine the population of the data collected for any experiment and consideration. In the first step, we will introduce the statistical hypothesis in R, and then cover the decision error in R, comprising one and two sample *t*-tests, and a *u*-test that entails a simple hypothesis and correlation. We will focus on covariance, comprising directional hypotheses, which is explained in a later section.

Statistical hypothesis in R

A statistical hypothesis is an assumption, or rather a presumption, made by the researcher about the data that is collected in relation to an experiment. This assumption does not have to be true every time. Hypothesis testing works only to validate the data.

Statistical hypotheses are categorized into two major types, and these are listed as follows:

- **Null hypothesis**: Where tests are used to check the validity of a particular claim. It is denoted as Ho.
- **Alternative hypothesis**: Where the null hypothesis concluded is usually considered to be untrue.

The steps that are applied to formulate a particular dataset in R are as follows:

1. State the hypothesis
2. Formulate a particular analysis plan
3. Analyze the given sample data
4. Interpret the results

In this section, we will focus on the following various hypothesis analyses that can be performed for our bank dataset.

The t-test in R

The student's t-test, also known as the t-test, is a method for comparing two samples. It can usually be implemented to determine whether the samples are linear or non-linear. This is regarded as a parametric test, and the data should normally be distributed.

 R can handle the various versions of the t-test using the t.test() command.

The following command is used to execute the loan eligibility of the given candidates in the bank dataset:

```
> t.test(bank$balance, bank$age)
Welch Two Sample t-test
data: bank$balance and bank$age
t = 48.717, df = 11161, p-value < 2.2e-16
alternative hypothesis: true difference in means is not equal to 0
95 percent confidence interval:
1427.464 1547.149
sample estimates:
mean of x mean of y
1528.53852 41.23195
```

This takes two parameters, namely, balance and age. The mandatory condition here is that both should be numeric parameters, which helps us to develop a hypothesis test in a systematic way.

The t.test() command is generally used to compare two vectors of numeric values. The vectors can be specified in a variety of ways, depending on how your data objects are set.

Directional hypothesis in R

Hypothesis testing includes a directional hypothesis, where a user can specify the direction for the dataset specified. The same function, with the alternative equal to (=) instruction, can switch the emphasis from a two-sided test (default) to a one-sided test. The alternatives are two.sided, less, or greater, and the choice can be abbreviated, as shown in the following command:

```
> t.test(bank$balance, mu = 5, alternative = 'greater')
One Sample t-test
data: bank$balance
t = 49.904, df = 11161, p-value < 2.2e-16
```

```
alternative hypothesis: true mean is greater than 5
95 percent confidence interval:
1478.318 Inf
sample estimates:
mean of x
1528.539
```

Consider the fact that we need to check the directional hypothesis of the balance of the candidates with our dataset as mentioned previously. The execution refers to 95 percent of the confidence interval, which is mandatory with respect to the p-value. The sample estimates refer to the mean of x, which is `1528.539`.

Correlation in R

The `cor()` command is used to determine correlations between two vectors, all of the columns of a data frame, or two data frames. The `cov()` command, on the other hand, examines covariance. The `cor.test()` command carries out a test as to the significance of the correlation.

Simple correlations are between two continuous variables and use the `cor()` command to obtain a correlation coefficient, as shown in the following command:

```
> cor(bank$balance, bank$age, method = 'spearman')
[1] 0.105988
```

The preceding example uses the Spearman Rho correlation, but a user can also apply Kendall's Tau by specifying `kendall` as the `method`:

```
> cor(bank$balance, bank$age, method = 'kendall')
[1] 0.07119334
```

A correlation is nothing but a bivariate analysis that measures the strength of association with respect to two variables and the direction of the relationship. It measures the strength of the relationship between the value of the correlation coefficient that varies between the range of +1 and -1.

Tietjen-Moore test

The Tietjen-Moore test algorithm is a generalization of the Grubbs' test algorithm, which is basically used for univariate datasets. The following algorithm depicts the detection of the multiple outliers in a univariate dataset by applying the Tietjen-Moore test algorithm. The following are the parameters used:

- **Input parameter**: Input data, including outliers
- **Output parameters**: Original data with outliers marked

The workflow is shown as follows:

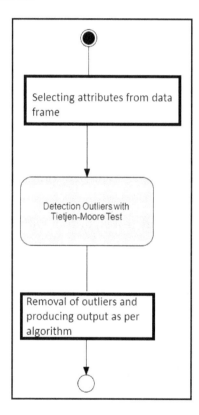

The step-wise approach will help us to create the function in the desired way. We will carry out the following steps to implement the detection of outliers in R for the bank dataset:

1. Create a function that assists in generating the outliers in R:

```
> TietjenMoore <- function(dataSeries,k)
+ {
+ n = length(dataSeries)
+ ## Compute the absolute residuals.
+ r = abs(dataSeries - mean(dataSeries))
+ ## Sort data according to size of residual.
+ df = data.frame(dataSeries,r)
+ dfs = df[order(df$r),]
+ ## Create a subset of the data without the largest k values.
+ klarge = c((n-k+1):n)
+ subdataSeries = dfs$dataSeries[-klarge]
+ ## Compute the sums of squares.
+ ksub = (subdataSeries - mean(subdataSeries))**2
+ all = (df$dataSeries - mean(df$dataSeries))**2
+ ## Compute the test statistic.
+ sum(ksub)/sum(all)
+ }
```

The function helps to compute the absolute residuals and sorts data according to the size of the residual. Later, we will focus on the computation of the sum of squares.

2. Implement the Tietjen-Moore test algorithm with the following function:

```
> FindOutliersTietjenMooreTest <-
function(dataSeries,k,alpha=0.05){
+ ek <- TietjenMoore(dataSeries,k)
+ ## Compute critical value based on simulation.
+ test = c(1:10000)
+ for (i in 1:10000){
+ dataSeriesdataSeries = rnorm(length(dataSeries))
+ test[i] = TietjenMoore(dataSeriesdataSeries,k) }
+ Talpha=quantile(test,alpha)
+ list(T=ek,Talpha=Talpha)
+ }
```

This function helps us to compute the critical value based on the simulation of data.

3. Now, let's demonstrate these functions with sample data and the bank dataset for evaluating the Tietjen-Moore test algorithm:

```
> x <- c(-1.40, -0.44, -0.30, -0.24, -0.22, -0.13, -0.05, 0.06,
0.10, 0.18,

+
0.20, 0.39, 0.48, 0.63, 1.01)

> FindOutliersTietjenMooreTest(x, 2)

$`T`
[1] 0.2919994

$Talpha
5%
0.3136918

> FindOutliersTietjenMooreTest(bank$balance, 2)
$`T`
[1] 0.8906338

$Talpha
5%
0.9966432
```

The evaluation returns the position of the values outside the permitted range by a criterion based on the Tietjen-Moore test algorithm.

Parsimonious models

Parsimonious models are simple models with great explanatory predictive power. They usually explain data with a minimum number of parameters, or predictor variables. MoEClust is the required R package that fits the finite Gaussian mixtures of experts' models. It uses a range of parsimonious covariance with the help of EM/CEM algorithms.

The steps to be carried out to perform parsimonious data analysis are as follows:

1. It is important to install the requisite package for parsimonious model creation of our bank dataset as follows:

```
> install.packages('devtools')
 Installing package into 'C:/Users/Radhika/Documents/R/win-
library/3.5'
 (as 'lib' is unspecified)
```

```
 trying URL
 'https://cran.rstudio.com/bin/windows/contrib/3.5/devtools_2.0.2.zi
 p'
 Content type 'application/zip' length 383720 bytes (374 KB)
 downloaded 374 KB
 package 'devtools' successfully unpacked and MD5 sums checked
 The downloaded binary packages are in
 C:\Users\Radhika\AppData\Local\Temp\Rtmpc1oW5p\downloaded_packages
 > install.packages('MoEClust')
 Installing package into 'C:/Users/Radhika/Documents/R/win-
 library/3.5'
 (as 'lib' is unspecified)
 trying URL
 'https://cran.rstudio.com/bin/windows/contrib/3.5/MoEClust_1.2.1.zi
 p'
 Content type 'application/zip' length 759555 bytes (741 KB)
 downloaded 741 KB
 package 'MoEClust' successfully unpacked and MD5 sums checked
 The downloaded binary packages are in
 C:\Users\Radhika\AppData\Local\Temp\Rtmpc1oW5p\downloaded_packages
 > library(MoEClust)

  ___   _        ____  ____  _  _
 |  \/  |       |  __/ _  \ | | | | Gaussian Parsimonious
 | .  . |  ___  | |_  | / \/ |_ _ ___| |_ Clustering Models
 | |\/| |/ _ \| __|| | | | | | / __| __| with Covariates
 | |  | | (_) | |__| \__/\ | |_| \__ \ |_
 \_| |_/\___/\____/ \____/_|\__,_|___/\__| version 1.2.1

 Type '?MoEClust' to see a brief guide to how to use this R
 package.
 Type 'citation("MoEClust")' for citing the package in
 publications.
 Type 'MoE_news()' to see new features recent changes and bug
 fixes.
 Warning message:
 package 'MoEClust' was built under R version 3.5.3
```

The preceding package specified helps to cluster the data as per the required value analysis.

2. Create separate data variables that evaluate the bank balance with respect to the parsimonious model:

```
> View(bank)
> age <- bank[,1]
> age

 [1] 59 56 41 55 54 42 56 60 37 28 38 30 29 46 31 35 32 49 41 49 28
```

```
43 43 43 37 35 31 43 31

[30] 28 32 60 26 40 33 32 35 33 38 23 60 48 45 36 52 35 43 52 53
48 41 39 59 41 48 40 48 60

[59] 40 57 51 41 41 52 59 44 49 40 41 44 60 29 41 41 42 36 39 31
26 31 29 37 33 24 50 27 54

[88] 30 34 37 41 47 31 31 43 37 30 41 36 35 29 35 31 35 34 31 44
36 35 41 31 34 32 36 30 37
```

3. For models that covariate in the gating network, or models with equal mixing
   proportions, there is no need to fit single component models:

```
> m1 <- MoE_clust(balance, G=0:2, verbose=FALSE)
> m1

Call: MoE_clust(data = balance, G = 0:2, verbose = FALSE)

Best Model (according to BIC): univariate, unequal variance (V),
with 2 components

BIC = -194528.759 | ICL = -195948.85 | AIC = -194492.158

No covariates

> m2 <- MoE_clust(balance, G=2, verbose=FALSE)
> m2

Call: MoE_clust(data = balance, G = 2, verbose = FALSE)

Best Model (according to BIC): univariate, unequal variance (V),
with 2 components

BIC = -194528.759 | ICL = -195948.85 | AIC = -194492.158

No covariates

> m3 <- MoE_clust(balance, G=1:2, verbose=FALSE)
```

4. Compare the data values with the requisite covariates:

```
> comp
```

```
--------------------------------------------------------------------
-----------

 Comparison of Gaussian Parsimonious Clustering Models with
 Covariates

 Data: balance

--------------------------------------------------------------------
-----------

 rank MoENames modelNames G df iters bic icl aic loglik gating

 1 m1 V 2 5 61 -194528.759 -195948.85 -194492.158 -97241.079 None

 2 m2 V 2 5 61 -194528.759 -195948.85 -194492.158 -97241.079 None

 3 m3 V 2 5 61 -194528.759 -195948.85 -194492.158 -97241.079 None

 expert equalPro

 None FALSE
 None FALSE
 None FALSE
```

5. A comparison of the balance parameter value with other values is effected with the help of plots that are required for data visualization:

```
> plot(comp$optimal, what="gpairs", jitter=FALSE)
```

This gives us the following plot:

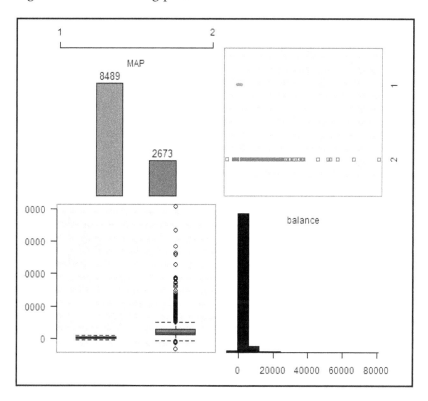

6. Convert the MoEClust class to the Mclust class in order to visualize the results with respect to the two options required:

```
> (mod <- as.Mclust(comp$optimal))

'Mclust' model object: (V,2)

Available components:

[1] "call" "data" "modelName" "n" "d"

[6] "G" "BIC" "bic" "loglik" "df"

[11] "hypvol" "parameters" "z" "classification" "uncertainty"

> plot(mod, what="classification")

> plot(mod, what="uncertainty")
```

The two plots generated are depicted as follows:

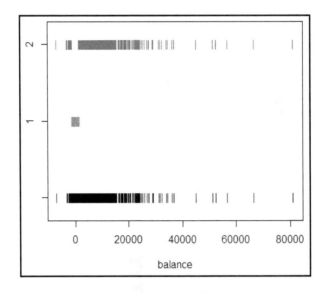

The balance is concentrated to a specific region that is clearly visible. This helps in checking the loan eligibility parameter very easily. The same can be visualized with the following plot:

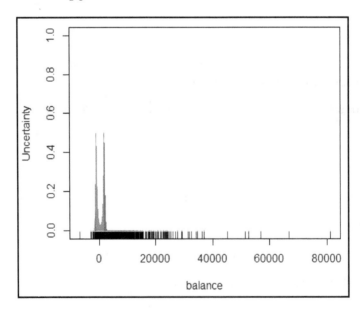

This plot helps to create uncertainty relating to the data in terms of the specific region and bandwidth. Now, we can focus on the probability plots, which will help us to gather the information relating to the `age`, `balance`, and `loan` parameters so as to check the loan eligibility.

Probability plots

This section describes the creation of probability plots in R that can be used for didactic purposes and, predominantly, for the purpose of data analysis. The following functions are available for each distribution of probability plots in the format specified:

Name	Description
dnorm()	Density or probability function
pnorm()	Cumulative density function
qnorm()	Quantile function
Rnorm()	Random deviates

We will be creating probability plots for the bank dataset with reference to the `age` and `balance` parameters, which are regarded as the crucial parameters in establishing loan eligibility using the following steps:

1. Include the library within the R workspace. This is considered a mandatory step:

```
> library(ggplot2)
Attaching package: 'ggplot2'
The following object is masked _by_ '.GlobalEnv':
mpg
Warning message:
package 'ggplot2' was built under R version 3.5.3
```

2. Use the probability plot functions (for each one of them) and their output with respect to the screenshots as follows:

```
> p1 <- ggplot(data = bank, aes(bank$balance)) + stat_function(fun
= dnorm, n = 101, args = list(mean =
0, sd = 1)) + ylab("") + scale_y_continuous(breaks = NULL)

> p1
```

This gives us the following plot:

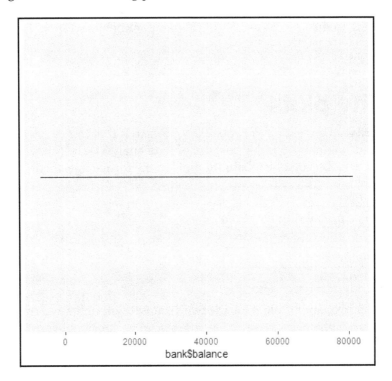

The line depicts the visualization in the specific manner, meaning that there is no variation with respect to the balance parameter. All that can be said is that it is concentrated toward a specific range.

3. The pnorm() function follows the same constraint, the only difference being the generation of random numbers with reference to the cumulative density function. We can demonstrate the pnorm() function by executing the following command:

```
> p2 <- ggplot(data = bank, aes(bank$balance)) +stat_function(fun =
pnorm, n = 101, args = list(mean = 0, sd = 1)) + ylab("") +
scale_y_continuous(breaks = NULL)

> p2
```

The visualization changes automatically, as shown in the following screenshot:

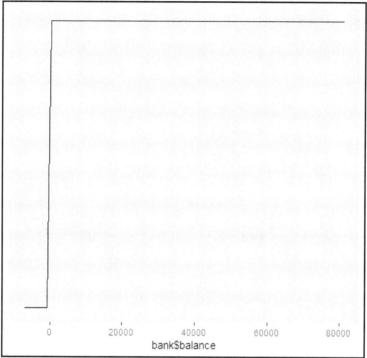

4. The `rnorm()` function generates a random value from the normal distribution with the standard syntax as follows:

```
> rnorm(n, mean = , sd = )
```

5. This is used to generate normal random numbers with the `mean` and `sd`, arguments. For our dataset, we can execute the following command to observe the probability curve as follows:

```
> p4 <- ggplot(data = bank, aes(bank$balance)) +
+
stat_function(fun = rnorm, n = 101, args = list(mean = 0, sd = 1))
+ ylab("") +scale_y_continuous(breaks = NULL)

> p4
```

The variation in the probability plot is now completely different compared to the previous ones. This is clearly visible in the following screenshot:

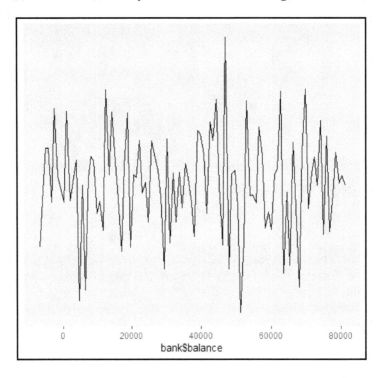

The Shapiro-Wilk test

shapiro.test tests the null hypothesis that *the samples come from a normal distribution*, vis-à-vis the alternative hypothesis, that *the samples do not come from a normal distribution*. Let's understand this in detail by executing the following command:

```
> ?shapiro.test
```

The R help page will be visible to users as follows:

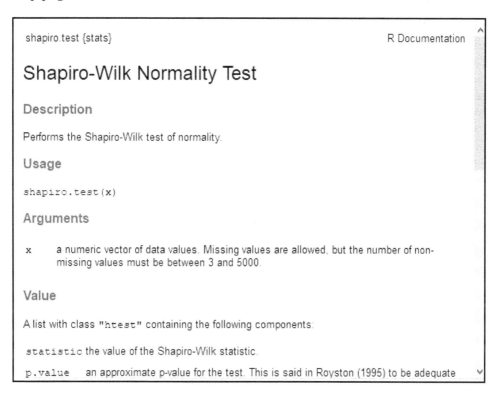

shapiro.test {stats}   R Documentation

Shapiro-Wilk Normality Test

Description

Performs the Shapiro-Wilk test of normality.

Usage

```
shapiro.test(x)
```

Arguments

x   a numeric vector of data values. Missing values are allowed, but the number of non-missing values must be between 3 and 5000.

Value

A list with class `"htest"` containing the following components:

`statistic` the value of the Shapiro-Wilk statistic.

`p.value`   an approximate p-value for the test. This is said in Royston (1995) to be adequate

We can see that it takes an argument of a numeric vector of data values from a specific range. Since we have implemented a data frame, it is mandatory to pass the desired column as input to this function. Consider creating a `shapiro.test` analysis for a `balance` attribute, as this is considered a critical attribute:

```
> shapiro.test(bank$balance[1:10])
Shapiro-Wilk normality test
data: bank$balance[1:10]
W = 0.80236, p-value = 0.01549
> shapiro.test(bank$balance[1:4000])
Shapiro-Wilk normality test
data: bank$balance[1:4000]
W = 0.45537, p-value < 2.2e-16
```

This means that if your *p-value* <= *0.05,* then you would *reject* the null hypothesis that the samples came from a normal distribution. As we increase the range, however, the *p*-value increases, satisfying the null hypothesis for the samples that form a normal distribution.

Summary

In this chapter, we have focused on the implementation of all the libraries discussed in previous chapters, which will help in evaluating the univariate dataset. The best demonstration of the univariate dataset was the loan eligibility parameter of the customer, which we implemented through various algorithms. We have listed some of the various packages that are available for reading, in various kinds of attributes, within the dataset mentioned in R. There are lots of different options, and even the options we have listed have a wide functionality that we are going to cover and use as we progress through the book. In this chapter, we understood the structure of the data after cleaning and tidying it up. We then covered various tests, such as the hypothesis test, the Tietjen-Moore test, and the parsimonious model. In the next chapter, we will introduce a time series dataset and look at how to use exploratory data analysis techniques to analyze the data.

Time Series Datasets 7

This chapter will introduce a time series dataset and help us to understand how to use EDA techniques to analyze the data. We will also learn about and use EDA techniques using an autocorrelation plot, spectrum plot, complex demodulation amplitude plot, and phase plots. In this chapter, we will first learn how to read and tidy up the data, after which we will learn how to map and understand the underlying structure of the dataset, and identify the important variables. We will then learn how to create a list of outliers or other anomalies using Grubbs' test. We will also cover the parsimonious model and Bartlett's test.

The following topics will be covered in this chapter:

- Introducing and reading in the data
- Cleaning and tidying up the data
- Mapping and understanding the underlying structure of the dataset, and identifying the most important variables
- Testing assumptions and hypotheses, estimating parameters, and establishing the margins of error
- Using Grubbs' test to create a list of outliers or other anomalies
- Uncovering a parsimonious model
- Measuring scale using Bartlett's test
- Exploring the dataset graphically using an autocorrelation plot, a spectrum plot, a complex demodulation amplitude plot, and a phase plot
- Summarizing our findings

Technical requirements

You should have hands-on experience or knowledge of the following points before getting started with this chapter:

- R programming language
- RStudio
- R packages
  (including `readr`, `readxl`, `jsonlite`, `httr`, `rvest`, `DBI`, `dplyr`, `stringr`, `forcats`, `lubridate`, `hms`, `blob`, `ggplot2`, and `knitr`)

Introducing and reading the dataset

In this chapter, we will focus on the dataset that consists of the responses of a gas with the help of a multi-sensor device. The dataset includes an hourly response average, which is being recorded along with gas concentrations and proportions. This dataset is referred to as an **Air Quality Dataset**.

You can download the file from the following link:

`https://github.com/PacktPublishing/Hands-On-Exploratory-Data-Analysis-with-R/tree/master/ch07`.

For more information, you can refer to the link specified as follows:
`https://archive.ics.uci.edu/ml/machine-learning-databases/00360/`.

In this section, we will be focusing on reading the attributes of the dataset and converting the `.csv` or `.xls` file to a data frame or dataset in the R workspace (with workspace, we are referring to the R environment where various data manipulations can be performed). As discussed in the previous chapters, we will be observing the following steps:

1. Include the necessary libraries for reading a particular dataset:

    ```
    > library(readr)
    > library(readxl)
    > AirQualityUCI <- read_xlsx("AirQualityUCI.xlsx")
    > View(AirQualityUCI)
    ```

The output generated is shown in the following screenshot:

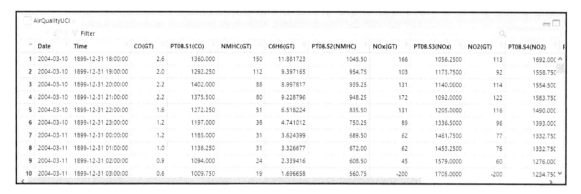

The attributes included previously are described in the following table:

Date	The tracked date represented in (DD/MM/YYYY) format.
Time	The time, which is tracked and represented as (HH.MM.SS).
CO(GT)	The actual average hourly concentration of CO in mg/m^3.
PT08.S1(CO)	$PT08.S1$ (tin oxide) average hourly sensor response (nominally CO targeted).
NMHC(GT)	The actual average hourly overall non-metallic hydrocarbon concentration in microg/m^3.
C6H6(GT)	The actual average hourly benzene concentration in microg/m^3.
PT08.S2(NMHC)	$PT08.S2$ (titania) average hourly sensor response.
NOx(GT) PT08.S3(NOx)	The actual average hourly NOx concentration in ppb. $PT08.S3$ (tungsten oxide) average hourly sensor response.
NO2(GT)	The actual average hourly $NO2$ concentration in microg/m^3.
PT08.S4(NO2)	$PT08.S4$ (tungsten oxide) average hourly sensor response.
PT08.S5(O3)	$PT08.S5$ (indium oxide) average hourly sensor response.
T	Temperature in °C.
RH	Relative humidity (%).
AH	Absolute humidity.

2. This step involves checking the various data types in our dataset by executing the following command:

```
> str(AirQualityUCI)
Classes 'tbl_df', 'tbl' and 'data.frame':    9357 obs. of   15
variables:
 $ Date         : POSIXct, format: "2004-03-10" "2004-03-10"
"2004-03-10" "2004-03-10" ...
 $ Time         : POSIXct, format: "1899-12-31 18:00:00"
"1899-12-31 19:00:00" "1899-12-31 20:00:00" "1899-12-31 21:00:00"
...
 $ CO(GT)       : num  2.6 2 2.2 2.2 1.6 1.2 1.2 1 0.9 0.6 ...
 $ PT08.S1(CO)  : num  1360 1292 1402 1376 1272 ...
 $ NMHC(GT)     : num  150 112 88 80 51 38 31 31 24 19 ...
 $ C6H6(GT)     : num  11.88 9.4 9 9.23 6.52 ...
 $ PT08.S2(NMHC): num  1046 955 939 948 836 ...
 $ NOx(GT)      : num  166 103 131 172 131 89 62 62 45 -200 ...
 $ PT08.S3(NOx) : num  1056 1174 1140 1092 1205 ...
 $ NO2(GT)      : num  113 92 114 122 116 96 77 76 60 -200 ...
 $ PT08.S4(NO2) : num  1692 1559 1554 1584 1490 ...
 $ PT08.S5(O3)  : num  1268 972 1074 1203 1110 ...
 $ T            : num  13.6 13.3 11.9 11 11.2 ...
 $ RH           : num  48.9 47.7 54 60 59.6 ...
 $ AH           : num  0.758 0.725 0.75 0.787 0.789 ...
```

Cleaning the dataset

Data cleaning, or tidying up the data, is the process of transforming raw data into a specific form of consistent data, which includes analysis in a simple manner. The R programming language includes a set of comprehensive tools that are specifically designed to clean the data in an effective manner. We will be focusing on cleaning the dataset here in a specific way by observing the following steps:

1. Include the libraries that are required to clean and tidy up the dataset:

```
> library(dplyr)
> library(tidyr)
```

2. Analyze the summary of our dataset, which will help us to focus on the attributes we need to work on:

```
> summary(AirQualityUCI)
      Date                     Time
CO(GT)          PT08.S1(CO)        NMHC(GT)
 Min.   :2004-03-10 00:00:00   Min.   :1899-12-31 00:00:00   Min.
 :-200.00   Min.    :-200   Min.    :-200.0
 1st Qu.:2004-06-16 00:00:00   1st Qu.:1899-12-31 05:00:00   1st
 Qu.:   0.60   1st Qu.: 921   1st Qu.:-200.0
 Median :2004-09-21 00:00:00   Median :1899-12-31 11:00:00   Median
 :   1.50   Median :1052   Median :-200.0
 Mean   :2004-09-21 04:30:05   Mean   :1899-12-31 11:29:55   Mean
 : -34.21   Mean    :1049   Mean    :-159.1
 3rd Qu.:2004-12-28 00:00:00   3rd Qu.:1899-12-31 18:00:00   3rd
 Qu.:   2.60   3rd Qu.:1221   3rd Qu.:-200.0
 Max.   :2005-04-04 00:00:00   Max.   :1899-12-31 23:00:00   Max.
 :  11.90   Max.    :2040   Max.    :1189.0
     C6H6(GT)        PT08.S2(NMHC)        NOx(GT)        PT08.S3(NOx)
NO2(GT)         PT08.S4(NO2)
 Min.   :-200.000   Min.    :-200.0   Min.    :-200.0   Min.
 :-200.0   Min.    :-200.00   Min.    :-200
 1st Qu.:   4.005   1st Qu.: 711.0   1st Qu.:  50.0   1st Qu.:
637.0   1st Qu.:  53.00   1st Qu.:1185
 Median :   7.887   Median : 894.5   Median : 141.0   Median :
794.2   Median :  96.00   Median :1446
 Mean   :   1.866   Mean    : 894.5   Mean    : 168.6   Mean    :
794.9   Mean    :  58.14   Mean    :1391
```

We need to focus on the data types such as (numeric, or character) included within the dataset, as shown previously.

3. This step involves checking the various data types of our dataset by executing the following command:

```
> str(AirQualityUCI)
Classes 'tbl_df', 'tbl' and 'data.frame':    9357 obs. of  15
variables:
 $ Date         : POSIXct, format: "2004-03-10" "2004-03-10"
"2004-03-10" "2004-03-10" ...
 $ Time         : POSIXct, format: "1899-12-31 18:00:00"
"1899-12-31 19:00:00" "1899-12-31 20:00:00" "1899-12-31 21:00:00"
...
 $ CO(GT)       : num  2.6 2 2.2 2.2 1.6 1.2 1.2 1 0.9 0.6 ...
 $ PT08.S1(CO)  : num  1360 1292 1402 1376 1272 ...
 $ NMHC(GT)     : num  150 112 88 80 51 38 31 31 24 19 ...
 $ C6H6(GT)     : num  11.88 9.4 9 9.23 6.52 ...
 $ PT08.S2(NMHC): num  1046 955 939 948 836 ...
```

```
$ NOx(GT)       : num   166 103 131 172 131 89 62 62 45 -200 ...
$ PT08.S3(NOx)  : num   1056 1174 1140 1092 1205 ...
$ NO2(GT)       : num   113 92 114 122 116 96 77 76 60 -200 ...
$ PT08.S4(NO2)  : num   1692 1559 1554 1584 1490 ...
$ PT08.S5(O3)   : num   1268 972 1074 1203 1110 ...
$ T             : num   13.6 13.3 11.9 11 11.2 ...
$ RH            : num   48.9 47.7 54 60 59.6 ...
$ AH            : num   0.758 0.725 0.75 0.787 0.789 ...
```

4. Now, let's view the first six columns and the last six columns of our data by executing the following command:

```
> head(AirQualityUCI)
# A tibble: 6 x 15
   Date                Time                    `CO(GT)`  `PT08.S1(CO)`
`NMHC(GT)` `C6H6(GT)`
   <dttm>              <dttm>                  <dbl>     <dbl>
<dbl>      <dbl>
1 2004-03-10 00:00:00 1899-12-31 18:00:00     2.6       1360
150     11.9
2 2004-03-10 00:00:00 1899-12-31 19:00:00     2         1292.
112      9.40
3 2004-03-10 00:00:00 1899-12-31 20:00:00     2.2       1402
88       9.00
4 2004-03-10 00:00:00 1899-12-31 21:00:00     2.2       1376.
80       9.23
5 2004-03-10 00:00:00 1899-12-31 22:00:00     1.6       1272.
51       6.52
6 2004-03-10 00:00:00 1899-12-31 23:00:00     1.2       1197
38       4.74
# ... with 9 more variables: `PT08.S2(NMHC)` <dbl>, `NOx(GT)`
<dbl>, `PT08.S3(NOx)` <dbl>,
#    `NO2(GT)` <dbl>, `PT08.S4(NO2)` <dbl>, `PT08.S5(O3)` <dbl>, T
<dbl>, RH <dbl>,
#    AH <dbl>
```

Similarly, we will use the following command to view the last six columns of our data:

```
> tail(AirQualityUCI)
# A tibble: 6 x 15
   Date                Time                    `CO(GT)`  `PT08.S1(CO)`
`NMHC(GT)` `C6H6(GT)`
   <dttm>              <dttm>                  <dbl>     <dbl>
<dbl>      <dbl>
1 2005-04-04 00:00:00 1899-12-31 09:00:00     3.9       1296.
-200     13.6
2 2005-04-04 00:00:00 1899-12-31 10:00:00     3.1       1314.
```

```
-200        13.5
3 2005-04-04 00:00:00 1899-12-31 11:00:00        2.4          1162.
-200        11.4
4 2005-04-04 00:00:00 1899-12-31 12:00:00        2.4          1142
-200        12.4
5 2005-04-04 00:00:00 1899-12-31 13:00:00        2.1          1002.
-200         9.55
6 2005-04-04 00:00:00 1899-12-31 14:00:00        2.2          1071.
-200        11.9
# ... with 9 more variables: `PT08.S2(NMHC)` <dbl>, `NOx(GT)`
<dbl>, `PT08.S3(NOx)` <dbl>,
#    `NO2(GT)` <dbl>, `PT08.S4(NO2)` <dbl>, `PT08.S5(O3)` <dbl>, T
<dbl>, RH <dbl>,
#    AH <dbl>
```

5. You can observe that other columns have the appropriate data type and the values associated with it, except for the time column. We need to import the necessary library to get the data in a specific format:

```
> library("lubridate")

Attaching package: 'lubridate'

The following object is masked from 'package:plyr':

    here

The following object is masked from 'package:base':

    date
```

The following command is executed to get only the time value extracted from the attribute:

```
> AirQualityUCI$Time<-parse_date_time(AirQualityUCI$Time,
orders="ymd hms")
```

This gives us the following output:

A	B
Date	Time
3/10/2004	18:00:00
3/10/2004	19:00:00
3/10/2004	20:00:00
3/10/2004	21:00:00
3/10/2004	22:00:00
3/10/2004	23:00:00
3/11/2004	0:00:00

6. After parsing the necessary attributes, it is important to use the tidying properties of R to unite the columns required, such as the date and time. This will help us to improve the analysis approach.

Mapping and understanding structure

This section involves understanding each and every attribute in depth, which is considered to be important for the dataset specified.

We need to carry out the following steps to understand the data structure and mapping attributes, if any:

1. Try to get a feel for the data as per the attribute structure:

```
> class(AirQualityUCI)
[1] "tbl_df"     "tbl"         "data.frame"
```

The output shows that the dataset is merely a tabular format of a data frame.

2. Check the dimensions of the dataset:

```
> dim(AirQualityUCI)
[1] 9357 15
```

This shows that the dataset comprises 9357 rows and 15 columns. The column structure has already been discussed in the first section.

3. View the column names of the dataset. We need to check whether these correspond to the records included in the Excel file:

```
> colnames(AirQualityUCI)
 [1] "Date" "Time" "CO(GT)" "PT08.S1(CO)" "NMHC(GT)"
 [6] "C6H6(GT)" "PT08.S2(NMHC)" "NOx(GT)" "PT08.S3(NOx)" "NO2(GT)"
[11] "PT08.S4(NO2)" "PT08.S5(O3)" "T"
```

4. Check the structure of the `AirQualityUCI` dataset by executing the following command:

```
> str(AirQualityUCI)
Classes 'tbl_df', 'tbl' and 'data.frame':    9357 obs. of   15
variables:
 $ Date       : POSIXct, format: "2004-03-10" "2004-03-10" ...
 $ Time       : POSIXct, format: "1899-12-31 18:00:00"
"1899-12-31 19:00:00" ...
 $ CO(GT)     : num  2.6 2 2.2 2.2 1.6 1.2 1.2 1 0.9 0.6 ...
```

```
$ PT08.S1(CO)    : num   1360 1292 1402 1376 1272 ...
$ NMHC(GT)       : num   150 112 88 80 51 38 31 31 24 19 ...
$ C6H6(GT)       : num   11.88 9.4 9 9.23 6.52 ...
$ PT08.S2(NMHC)  : num   1046 955 939 948 836 ...
$ NOx(GT)        : num   166 103 131 172 131 89 62 62 45 -200 ...
$ PT08.S3(NOx)   : num   1056 1174 1140 1092 1205 ...
$ NO2(GT)        : num   113 92 114 122 116 96 77 76 60 -200 ...
$ PT08.S4(NO2)   : num   1692 1559 1554 1584 1490 ...
$ PT08.S5(O3)    : num   1268 972 1074 1203 1110 ...
$ T              : num   13.6 13.3 11.9 11 11.2 ...
$ RH             : num   48.9 47.7 54 60 59.6 ...
$ AH             : num   0.758 0.725 0.75 0.787 0.789 ...
```

The structure depicts the data type of each column and the values associated with it, such as numeric or decimal format.

5. Check the structure using the dplyr package:

```
> library(dplyr)
>
> glimpse(AirQualityUCI)
Observations: 9,357
Variables: 15
$ Date           <dttm> 2004-03-10, 2004-03-10, 2004-03-10,
2004-03-10, 2004-03-10, 2...
$ Time           <dttm> 1899-12-31 18:00:00, 1899-12-31 19:00:00,
1899-12-31 20:00:00...
$ `CO(GT)`       <dbl> 2.6, 2.0, 2.2, 2.2, 1.6, 1.2, 1.2, 1.0,
0.9, 0.6, -200.0, 0.7,...
$ `PT08.S1(CO)`  <dbl> 1360.00, 1292.25, 1402.00, 1375.50,
1272.25, 1197.00, 1185.00,...
$ `NMHC(GT)`     <dbl> 150, 112, 88, 80, 51, 38, 31, 31, 24, 19,
14, 8, 16, 29, 64, 8...
$ `C6H6(GT)`     <dbl> 11.881723, 9.397165, 8.997817, 9.228796,
6.518224, 4.741012, 3...
$ `PT08.S2(NMHC)` <dbl> 1045.50, 954.75, 939.25, 948.25, 835.50,
750.25, 689.50, 672.0...
$ `NOx(GT)`      <dbl> 166, 103, 131, 172, 131, 89, 62, 62, 45,
-200, 21, 16, 34, 98,...
$ `PT08.S3(NOx)` <dbl> 1056.25, 1173.75, 1140.00, 1092.00,
1205.00, 1336.50, 1461.75,...
$ `NO2(GT)`      <dbl> 113, 92, 114, 122, 116, 96, 77, 76, 60,
-200, 34, 28, 48, 82, ...
```

`glimpse()` makes it possible to have a look at each and every column of the data frame. It is similar to `str()`, the only difference being that it displays more data than the `str()` function, which is normally used to obtain the structure of the data.

6. Plot the important parameters of our data frame, which focuses on calculating the percentage of pollution, namely, relative and absolute humidity:

```
> plot(AirQualityUCI$AH, AirQualityUCI$RH, main = "Humidity
Analysis", xlab = "Absolute Humidity", ylab = "Relative Humidity")
```

This gives us the following output:

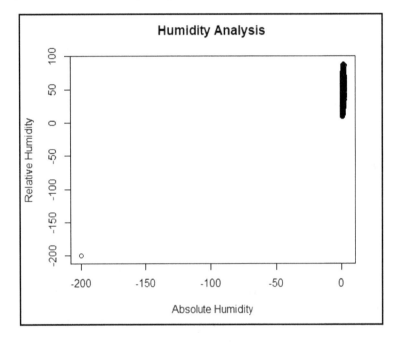

Hypothesis test

This section is all about hypothesis testing in R. This testing is merely an assumption made by the researcher regarding the population of data collected for any experiment. The first step entails an introduction to the statistical hypothesis in R, and later we will cover the decision error in R, which includes one- and two-sample t-tests, u-tests, correlation, and covariance in R.

t-test in R

This is also known as Student's t-test, which is a method for comparing two samples. It can usually be implemented to determine whether the samples are proper or different. This is considered as a parametric test, and the data should be normally distributed. R can handle the various versions of the t-test using the `t.test()` command.

The following command is used for our `AirQuality` dataset to check the parameters of relative and absolute humidity:

```
> t.test(AirQualityUCI$RH,   AirQualityUCI$AH)
   Welch Two Sample t-test
data:  AirQualityUCI$RH and   AirQualityUCI$AH
t = 69.62, df = 17471, p-value < 2.2e-16
alternative hypothesis: true difference   in means is not equal to 0
95 percent confidence interval:
 45.01707 47.62536
sample estimates:
mean of x mean of y
39.483611 -6.837604
```

The `t.test()` command is generally used to compare two vectors of numeric values. The vectors can be specified in a variety of ways, depending on how your data objects are set out.

Directional hypothesis in R

In hypothesis testing, you can only specify a direction to the dataset specified. Here, we will use the same function with the alternative equal to the (=) instruction to switch the emphasis from a two-sided test (default) to a one-sided test. The choices available to us are *two-sided*, *less*, or *greater*, and this choice can be abbreviated, as shown in the following command:

```
> t.test(AirQualityUCI$RH, mu = 5,   alternative = 'greater')
   One Sample t-test
data:  AirQualityUCI$RH
t = 65.13, df = 9356, p-value < 2.2e-16
alternative hypothesis: true mean is   greater than 5
95 percent confidence interval:
 38.61264      Inf
sample estimates:
mean of x
 39.48361
> t.test(AirQualityUCI$AH, mu = 5,   alternative = 'greater')
```

```
   One Sample t-test
data:  AirQualityUCI$AH
t = -29.378, df = 9356, p-value = 1
alternative hypothesis: true mean is   greater than 5
95 percent confidence interval:
 -7.500441       Inf
sample estimates:
mean of x
-6.837604
```

Grubbs' test and checking outliers

In R programming, an outlier is merely an observation that is unique in comparison with most of the other observations. An outlier is present because of errors in measurement in the data frame.

The following script is used to detect the particular outliers for each and every attribute:

```
> outlierKD <- function(dt, var) {
+     var_name <- eval(substitute(var),eval(dt))
+     na1 <- sum(is.na(var_name))
+     m1 <- mean(var_name, na.rm = T)
+     par(mfrow=c(2, 2), oma=c(0,0,3,0))
+     boxplot(var_name, main="With outliers")
+     hist(var_name, main="With outliers", xlab=NA, ylab=NA)
+     outlier <- boxplot.stats(var_name)$out
+     mo <- mean(outlier)
+     var_name <- ifelse(var_name %in% outlier, NA, var_name)
+     boxplot(var_name, main="Without outliers")
+     hist(var_name, main="Without outliers", xlab=NA, ylab=NA)
+     title("Outlier Check", outer=TRUE)
+     na2 <- sum(is.na(var_name))
+     cat("Outliers identified:", na2 - na1, "n")
+     cat("Propotion (%) of outliers:", round((na2 - na1) /
sum(!is.na(var_name))*100, 1), "n")
+     cat("Mean of the outliers:", round(mo, 2), "n")
+     m2 <- mean(var_name, na.rm = T)
+     cat("Mean without removing outliers:", round(m1, 2), "n")
+     cat("Mean if we remove outliers:", round(m2, 2), "n")
+     response <- readline(prompt="Do you want to remove outliers and to
replace with NA? [yes/no]: ")
+     if(response == "y" | response == "yes"){
+         dt[as.character(substitute(var))] <- invisible(var_name)
+         assign(as.character(as.list(match.call())$dt), dt, envir =
.GlobalEnv)
+         cat("Outliers successfully removed", "n")
```

```
+              return(invisible(dt))
+          } else{
+              cat("Nothing changed", "n")
+              return(invisible(var_name))
+          }
+      }
+   }
>   outlierKD(AirQualityUCI,AH)
```

For now, if we want to check the outliers for relative and absolute humidity, the preceding command is executed and the output generated is shown in the following diagram:

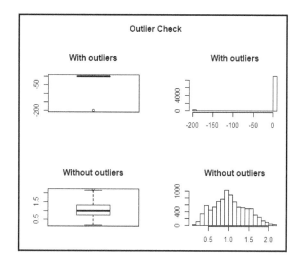

The following plot is created after the outliers are removed from the dataset:

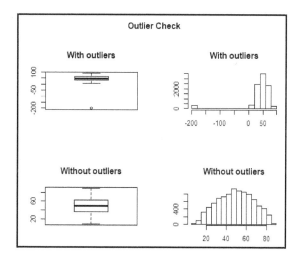

Grubbs' test is basically a test undertaken with statistics to identify the outliers in a univariate dataset that's assumed to come from a normally distributed population. The following steps are used to evaluate the data frame with the core attributes of AH and RH:

1. Install the `outliers` package, which helps to detect outliers for a specified column:

```
> install.packages("outliers") Installing package into
'C:/Users/Radhika/Documents/R/win-library/3.5' (as 'lib' is
unspecified) trying URL
'https://cran.rstudio.com/bin/windows/contrib/3.5/outliers_0.14.zip
' Content type 'application/zip' length 83897 bytes (81 KB)
downloaded 81 KB package 'outliers' successfully unpacked and MD5
sums checked The downloaded binary packages are in
C:\Users\Radhika\AppData\Local\Temp\Rtmpc1oW5p\downloaded_packages
```

2. Include the necessary libraries to calculate Grubbs' test:

```
> library(outliers) Warning message: package 'outliers' was built
under R version 3.5.2 > library(ggplot2)
```

3. Create a function for generating flag values of outliers. The following function follows Grubbs' test conditions:

```
> grubbs.flag <- function(x) {
+       outliers <- NULL
+       test <- x
+       grubbs.result <-    grubbs.test(test)
+       pv <- grubbs.result$p.value
+       while(pv < 0.05) {
+           outliers <-
c(outliers,as.numeric(strsplit(grubbs.result$alternative,"
")[[1]][3]))
+           test <- x[!x %in% outliers]
+           grubbs.result <-    grubbs.test(test)
+           pv <- grubbs.result$p.value
+       }
+       return(data.frame(X=x,Outlier=(x    %in% outliers)))
+ }
```

4. Call the `flag` function to analyze the value interpretation of AH and RH:

```
> grubbs.flag(AirQualityUCI$AH)
              X Outlier
1     0.7577538   FALSE
2     0.7254874   FALSE
3     0.7502391   FALSE
```

```
4        0.7867125    FALSE
5        0.7887942    FALSE
6        0.7847717    FALSE
7        0.7603119    FALSE
8        0.7702385    FALSE
9        0.7648187    FALSE
```

5. If you want a histogram with different colors, you can use the following command:

```
>ggplot(grubbs.flag(AirQualityUCI$AH),aes(x=AirQualityUCI$AH,color=
Outlier,fill=Outlier))
+        geom_histogram(binwidth=diff(range(AirQualityUCI$AH))/30)+
+        theme_bw()
```

This gives us the following output:

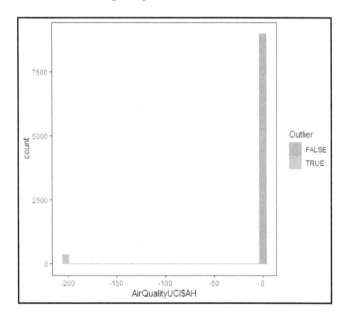

Parsimonious models

Parsimonious models are simple models with great explanatory predictive power. They usually explain data with a minimum number of parameters, or predictor variables. `MoEClust` is the R package that fits finite Gaussian mixtures of experts' models. It uses a range of parsimonious covariance with the help of EM or CEM algorithms.

Follow these steps to create a range of parsimonious covariance models with our `AirQualityUCI` dataset:

1. Install the package that is required to create a parsimonious model of our dataset:

```
> install.packages('devtools')
Installing package into 'C:/Users/Radhika/Documents/R/win-
library/3.5'
(as 'lib' is unspecified)
trying URL
'https://cran.rstudio.com/bin/windows/contrib/3.5/devtools_2.0.2.zi
p'
Content type 'application/zip' length 383720 bytes (374 KB)
downloaded 374 KB

package 'devtools' successfully unpacked and MD5 sums checked

The downloaded binary packages are in
C:\Users\Radhika\AppData\Local\Temp\Rtmpc1oW5p\downloaded_packages
```

2. The following step involves the installation of a package that assists in the creation of a parsimonious model:

```
> install.packages('MoEClust')
Installing package into 'C:/Users/Radhika/Documents/R/win-
library/3.5'
(as 'lib' is unspecified)
trying URL
'https://cran.rstudio.com/bin/windows/contrib/3.5/MoEClust_1.2.1.zi
p'
Content type 'application/zip' length 759555 bytes (741 KB)
downloaded 741 KB

package 'MoEClust' successfully unpacked and MD5 sums checked

The downloaded binary packages are in
C:\Users\Radhika\AppData\Local\Temp\Rtmpc1oW5p\downloaded_packages
> library(MoEClust)
```

```
Type '?MoEClust' to see a brief guide to how to use this R package.
Type 'citation("MoEClust")' for citing the package in publications.
```

```
Type 'MoE_news()' to see new features recent changes and bug fixes.

Warning message:
package 'MoEClust' was built under R version 3.5.3
```

This package helps to cluster the data as per the required value analysis.

3. Create separate data variables of the parameters of the `AirQualityUCI` dataset, which includes various gases responsible for pollution:

```
> View(AirQualityUCI)
> Date
# A tibble: 9,357 x 1
   Date
   <dttm>
 1 2004-03-10 00:00:00
 2 2004-03-10 00:00:00
 3 2004-03-10 00:00:00
 4 2004-03-10 00:00:00
 5 2004-03-10 00:00:00
 6 2004-03-10 00:00:00
 7 2004-03-11 00:00:00
 8 2004-03-11 00:00:00
 9 2004-03-11 00:00:00
10 2004-03-11 00:00:00
# ... with 9,347 more rows

> RH <-AirQualityUCI[,14]
> RH
# A tibble: 9,357 x 1
       RH
    <dbl>
 1   48.9
 2   47.7
 3   54.0
 4   60
 5   59.6
 6   59.2
 7   56.8
 8   60
 9   59.7
10   60.2
# ... with 9,347 more rows
> AH <-AirQualityUCI[,15]
> AH
# A tibble: 9,357 x 1
       AH
    <dbl>
```

```
 1 0.758
 2 0.725
 3 0.750
 4 0.787
 5 0.789
 6 0.785
 7 0.760
 8 0.770
 9 0.765
10 0.752
# ... with 9,347 more rows
```

4. For models that covariate in the gating network, or models with equal mixing proportions, there is no need to fit single component models:

```
> m1    <- MoE_clust(RH, G=0:2,   verbose=FALSE)
> m1
Call:   MoE_clust(data = RH, G = 0:2,   verbose = FALSE)
Best Model (according to BIC): univariate,   equal variance (E),
with 2 components
BIC = -82672.128 | ICL = -82672.128 | AIC   = -82643.553
No covariates
> m2    <- MoE_clust(RH, G=2,   verbose=FALSE)
> m2
Call:   MoE_clust(data = RH, G = 2,   verbose = FALSE)
Best Model (according to BIC):   univariate, equal variance (E),
with 2 components
BIC = -82672.128 | ICL = -82672.128 | AIC   = -82643.553
No covariates
```

5. This step involves a comparison of the data values with the required covariates:

```
> comp <- MoE_compare(m1, m2)
Warning: Ties for the optimal model exist according to the 'bic'
criterion: choosing the most parsimonious model

> comp
-----------------------------------------------------------------
-----------
Comparison of Gaussian Parsimonious Clustering Models with
Covariates
Data: RH
-----------------------------------------------------------------
-----------

 rank MoENames modelNames   G  df iters        bic        icl
aic      loglik
    1       m1          E   2   4     82 -82672.128 -82672.128
```

```
-82643.553 -41317.776
      2        m2              E    2    4    82 -82672.128 -82672.128
-82643.553 -41317.776
    NA      <NA>         <NA> <NA> <NA>  <NA>        <NA>        <NA>
  <NA>      <NA>
 gating expert equalPro
   None   None    FALSE
   None   None    FALSE
   <NA>   <NA>     <NA>
```

6. The value comparison of various parameters is executed with the help of other plots that are required for data visualization:

```
> plot(comp$optimal, what="gpairs",   jitter=FALSE)
```

This gives us the following output:

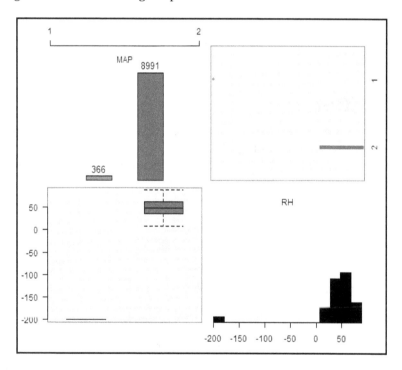

7. Convert the `MoEClust` class to the `Mclust` class in order to visualize the results, with respect to the two options that are required:

```
> (mod <- as.Mclust(comp$optimal))
'Mclust' model object: (E,2)
Available components:
```

```
     [1] "call"           "data"          "modelName"      "n"
     "d"
     [6] "G"              "BIC"           "bic"            "loglik"
     "df"
    [11] "hypvol"         "parameters"    "z"
    "classification" "uncertainty"
    > plot(mod, what="classification")
    > plot(mod, what="uncertainty")
```

The two plots describe the variation, which is generated as follows:

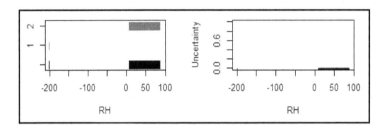

Bartlett's test

Bartlett's test is useful when executing a comparison between two or more samples to specify whether they are taken from populations with equal variance. Bartlett's test works successfully for normally distributed data. This test includes a null hypothesis, with a calculation of equal variances, and the alternative hypothesis, where variances are not considered equal. This test is considered useful for checking the assumptions regarding variance analysis.

The user can perform Bartlett's test with the `bartlett.test` function in R. The normal syntax for this is as follows :

```
> bartlett.test(values~groups, dataset)
```

Here, the parameters refer to the following:

- `values`: The name of the variable containing the data value
- `groups`: The name of the variable that specifies which sample each value belongs to

If the data is in an unstacked form (with the samples stored in separate variables), we need to implement the `list` function to evaluate Bartlett's test, demonstrated as follows:

```
> bartlett.test(list(dataset$sample1, dataset$sample2, dataset$sample3))
```

The following steps are implemented to perform Bartlett's test for our dataset, that is, `AirQualityUCI`:

1. Select the attributes for which you need to perform Bartlett's test:

```
> View(AirQualityUCI)
```

This gives us the following output:

	PT08.S2(NMHC)	NOx(GT)	PT08.S3(NOx)	NO2(GT)	PT08.S4(NO2)	PT08.S5(O3)	T	RH	AH
'23	1045.50	166	1056.2500	113	1692.000	1267.50	13.600000	48.87500	0.7577538
65	954.75	103	1173.7500	92	1558.750	972.25	13.300000	47.70000	0.7254874
÷17	939.25	131	1140.0000	114	1554.500	1074.00	11.900000	53.97500	0.7502391
'96	948.25	172	1092.0000	122	1583.750	1203.25	11.000000	60.00000	0.7867125
:24	835.50	131	1205.0000	116	1490.000	1110.00	11.150000	59.57500	0.7887942
÷12	750.25	89	1336.5000	96	1393.000	949.25	11.175000	59.17500	0.7847717
÷99	689.50	62	1461.7500	77	1332.750	732.50	11.325000	56.77500	0.7603119
÷77	672.00	62	1453.2500	76	1332.750	729.50	10.675000	60.00000	0.7702385
÷16	608.50	45	1579.0000	60	1276.000	619.50	10.650000	59.67500	0.7648187
÷58	560.75	-200	1705.0000	-200	1234.750	501.25	10.250000	60.20000	0.7516572

Showing 1 to 11 of 9,357 entries

Console ~/

```
> View(AirQualityUCI)
>
```

2. Perform Bartlett's test to analyze the pollution parameters with `RH` and `AH`:

```
> bartlett.test(RH~Date, AirQualityUCI)
    Bartlett test of homogeneity of   variances
data:  RH by Date
Bartlett's K-squared = Inf, df = 390, p-value   < 2.2e-16
> bartlett.test(AH~Date,   AirQualityUCI)
    Bartlett test of homogeneity of   variances
data:  AH by Date
Bartlett's K-squared = Inf, df = 390, p-value   < 2.2e-16
```

According to the output, the `p-value` is less than $2.2e-16$. However, it is not less than the significance level. The output refers to no rejection as per null hypothesis standards with a variance that is treated as equal.

Data visualization

In this section, we will focus on the creation of the following plots:

- Autocorrelation
- Spectrum
- Phase

Autocorrelation plots

Autocorrelation plots are regarded as plots for creating randomness in a particular dataset. This randomness is very powerful regarding autocorrelations of data values with varying time lags. It is mandatory that autocorrelations for any dataset should be near zero, for any and all time-lag separations.

The `Acf` function computes (and, by default, plots) an estimate of the autocorrelation function of a (possibly multivariate) time series. The syntax is as follows:

```
> Acf(x, lag.max = NULL, type = c("correlation", "covariance","partial"),
plot = TRUE, na.action = na.contiguous, demean = TRUE,
...)
```

The autocorrelation plot for our dataset with all of the 15 attributes is generated using the following command:

```
> acf(AirQualityUCI)
> acf(AirQualityUCI)
Hit <Return> to see next plot:
Hit <Return> to see next plot:
Hit <Return> to see next plot:
Hit <Return> to see next plot:
```

This describes all of the options that describe the randomness of data. The plot shown here has been created keeping those 15 attributes in mind:

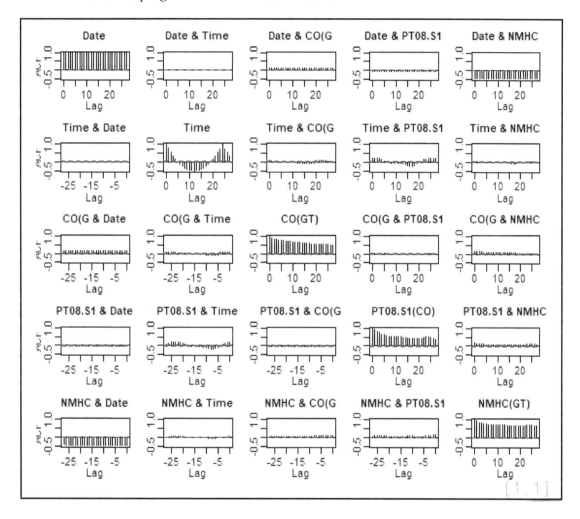

The following plot has been generated while retaining the first probability of the columns in our data frame:

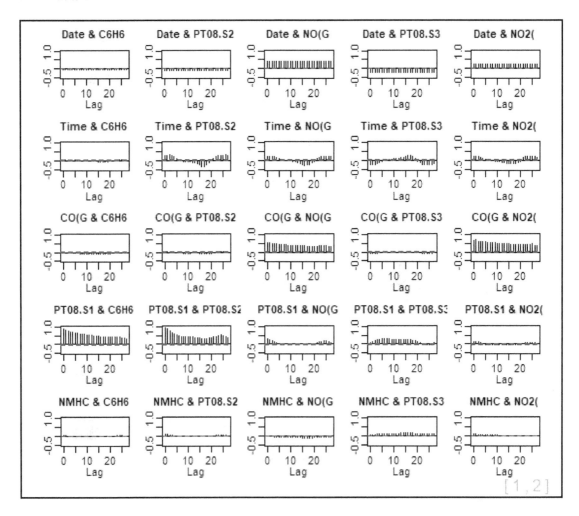

The following diagram refers to a second random combination that is generated:

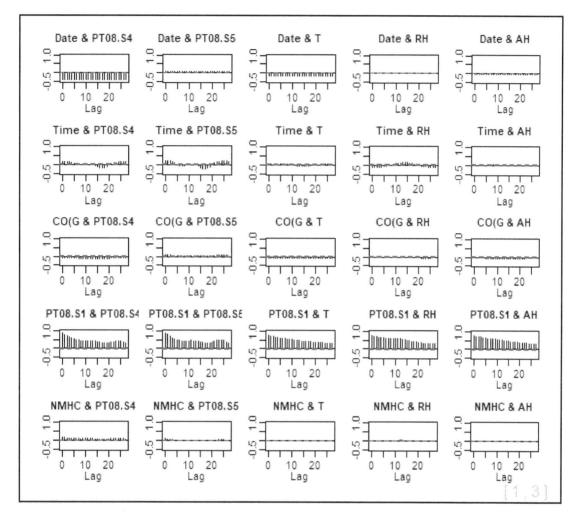

Each variation is depicted in a matrix form, which includes all the columns included in our data frame.

Spectrum plots

Spectrum plots generate spectral densities of the time series. We will implement the following steps to create spectrum plots for the dataset indicated. Spectrum plots create a separate variation with time series representations. The following syntax is used to create a spectrum plot:

```
spectrum(x, ..., method = c("pgram", "ar"))
```

Here, the parameters refer to the following:

- x: A univariate or multivariate time series.
- method: A string specifying the method used to estimate the spectral density. Permitted methods are pgram (the default) and ar, which can be abbreviated.

Now, let's create a spectral plot for our dataset. The spectral plots take all attributes together:

```
> require(graphics)
> spectrum(AirQualityUCI, method = c("pgram",    "ar"))
> spectrum(AirQualityUCI)
```

This gives us the following plot:

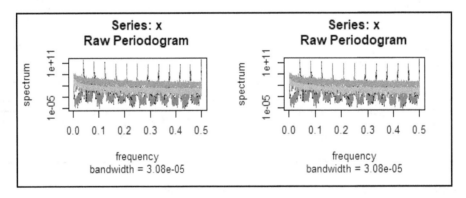

As you can see, the spectrum plot focuses on the frequency and bandwidth of the dataset with default values. The variations are depicted with a color range that automatically calls for a time series representation.

Phase plots

Phase plots return a 2D or 3D representation of a time wave according to its first, second, and possibly third derivatives.

The following steps are used to create phase plots with 2D or 3D representations for creating a particular phase plot. It is essential to create and install the requisite package such as seewave, which is mandatory:

1. Install the necessary packages to create phase plots:

```
> install.packages("seewave")
Installing package into 'C:/Users/Radhika/Documents/R/win-
library/3.5'
(as 'lib' is unspecified)
trying URL
'https://cran.rstudio.com/bin/windows/contrib/3.5/seewave_2.1.3.zip
'
Content type 'application/zip' length 3080821 bytes (2.9 MB)
downloaded 2.9 MB

package 'seewave' successfully unpacked and MD5 sums checked

The downloaded binary packages are in
C:\Users\Radhika\AppData\Local\Temp\Rtmpc1oW5p\downloaded_packages
> library(seewave)

Attaching package: 'seewave'

The following object is masked from 'package:lubridate':

    duration

The following object is masked from 'package:readr':

    spec

Warning message:
package 'seewave' was built under R version 3.5.3
```

2. Call for the phaseplot function with the required parameters. You can see the phase plot that is being created:

```
> phaseplot(AirQualityUCI, , dim = 2)
```

This gives us the following plot:

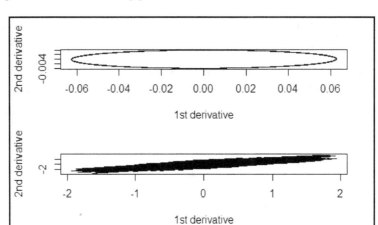

Summary

In this chapter, we focused on the implementation of all the libraries of a univariate dataset, which holds a strong representation for time series creation. The best illustration considered in this chapter is the measurement of pollution with respect to parsimonious models with RH and AH. We have listed some of the various packages that are available for reading, in various kinds of attributes, within the dataset indicated in R. There are lots of different options, and even the options we have listed have a wide functionality that we are going to cover and use as we progress through the book.

In the next chapter, we will cover multivariate datasets. Multivariate datasets include a combination of fixed and continuous variables that help us with further exploratory analysis.

8
Multivariate Datasets

This chapter will introduce a dataset from the multivariate problem category. We will learn how to use exploratory data analysis techniques to analyze this data. We will first learn to clean the data and understand the underlying structure of the dataset. We will cover the parsimonious model and Levene's test and then move on to data visualization. Following this, we will carry out exploratory data analysis on a real-world dataset called Longley's Economic Regression Data.

The following topics will be covered in this chapter:

- Introducing and reading data
- Cleaning and tidying up data
- Mapping and understanding the underlying structure of a dataset and identifying the most important variables
- Testing assumptions and hypotheses, estimating parameters, and calculating the margins of error
- Uncovering a parsimonious model
- Running a two-sample test for equal means
- Measuring scale using Levene's test
- Exploring the dataset graphically using the star plot, the scatter plot matrix, the conditioning plot, and principal component techniques

Technical requirements

You should have hands-on experience or knowledge of the following points before getting started with this chapter:

- R programming language
- RStudio
- R packages
  (including `readr`, `readxl`, `jsonlite`, `httr`, `rvest`, `DBI`, `dplyr`, `stringr`, `forcats`, `lubridate`, `hms`, `blob`, `ggplot2`, and `knitr`)

Introducing and reading a dataset

In this chapter, we will focus on a macroeconomic dataset that is found in a built-in library called `dataset` in R. It provides a well-known example of a highly collinear regression.

The data frame includes seven economical variables, observed yearly from 1947 to 1962 (*n=16*):

```
> library(pls)
> data(longley)
```

As discussed in previous chapters, we will carry out the following steps to read the data structure:

1. After including the necessary libraries, you can have a look at the attribute structure:

```
> longley
     GNP.deflator GNP Unemployed Armed.Forces Population Year Employed

1947 83.0 234.289 235.6 159.0 107.608 1947 60.323
1948 88.5 259.426 232.5 145.6 108.632 1948 61.122
1949 88.2 258.054 368.2 161.6 109.773 1949 60.171
1950 89.5 284.599 335.1 165.0 110.929 1950 61.187
1951 96.2 328.975 209.9 309.9 112.075 1951 63.221
1952 98.1 346.999 193.2 359.4 113.270 1952 63.639
1953 99.0 365.385 187.0 354.7 115.094 1953 64.989
1954 100.0 363.112 357.8 335.0 116.219 1954 63.761
1955 101.2 397.469 290.4 304.8 117.388 1955 66.019
1956 104.6 419.180 282.2 285.7 118.734 1956 67.857
1957 108.4 442.769 293.6 279.8 120.445 1957 68.169
1958 110.8 444.546 468.1 263.7 121.950 1958 66.513
```

```
1959 112.6 482.704 381.3 255.2 123.366 1959 68.655
1960 114.2 502.601 393.1 251.4 125.368 1960 69.564
1961 115.7 518.173 480.6 257.2 127.852 1961 69.331
1962 116.9 554.894 400.7 282.7 130.081 1962 70.551
```

2. You can look at the dataset with the help of the `View` command:

```
> View(longley)
```

From here, we get the following output:

	GNP.deflator	GNP	Unemployed	Armed.Forces	Population	Year	Employed
1947	83.0	234.289	235.6	159.0	107.608	1947	60.323
1948	88.5	259.426	232.5	145.6	108.632	1948	61.122
1949	88.2	258.054	368.2	161.6	109.773	1949	60.171
1950	89.5	284.599	335.1	165.0	110.929	1950	61.187
1951	96.2	328.975	209.9	309.9	112.075	1951	63.221
1952	98.1	346.999	193.2	359.4	113.270	1952	63.639
1953	99.0	365.385	187.0	354.7	115.094	1953	64.989
1954	100.0	363.112	357.8	335.0	116.219	1954	63.761
1955	101.2	397.469	290.4	304.8	117.388	1955	66.019
1956	104.6	419.180	282.2	285.7	118.734	1956	67.857

Showing 1 to 11 of 16 entries

3. We need to now focus on the structure of the data frame with the requisite function:

```
> str(longley)
'data.frame': 16 obs. of 7 variables:

$ GNP.deflator: num 83 88.5 88.2 89.5 96.2 ...
$ GNP : num 234 259 258 285 329 ...
$ Unemployed : num 236 232 368 335 210 ...
$ Armed.Forces: num 159 146 162 165 310 ...
$ Population : num 108 109 110 111 112 ...
$ Year : int 1947 1948 1949 1950 1951 1952 1953 1954 1955 1956 ...
$ Employed : num 60.3 61.1 60.2 61.2 63.2 ...
```

Let's discuss the attribute names and their description in our dataset:

Attribute	Description
GNP.deflator	GNP implicit price deflator (*1954=100*)
GNP	Gross National Product
Unemployed	Number of unemployed people
Armed.Forces	Number of people in the armed forces
Population	Non-institutionalized population ≥ 14 years of age
Year	The year (time)
Employed	Number of people employed

Cleaning the data

Data cleaning, or rather tidying up the data, is the process of transforming raw data into specific consistent data that includes analysis in a simpler manner. The R programming language includes a set of comprehensive tools that are specifically designed to clean the data in an effective manner. We will be focusing here on cleaning the dataset in a specific way:

1. Include the libraries that are needed for cleaning and tidying up the dataset:

    ```
    > library(dplyr)
    > library(tidyr)
    ```

2. Analyze the summary of our dataset, which will help us to focus on which attributes to use:

    ```
    >summary(longley)
      GNP Deflator GNP Unemployed Armed Forces Population Year Employed
     Min. : 83.00 Min. :234.3 Min. :187.0 Min. :145.6 Min. :107.6 Min.
     :1947 Min. :60.17
     1st Qu.: 94.53 1st Qu.:317.9 1st Qu.:234.8 1st Qu.:229.8 1st
     Qu.:111.8 1st Qu.:1951 1st Qu.:62.71
     Median :100.60 Median :381.4 Median :314.4 Median :271.8 Median
     :116.8 Median :1954 Median :65.50
     Mean :101.68 Mean :387.7 Mean :319.3 Mean :260.7 Mean :117.4 Mean
     :1954 Mean :65.32
     3rd Qu.:111.25 3rd Qu.:454.1 3rd Qu.:384.2 3rd Qu.:306.1 3rd
     Qu.:122.3 3rd Qu.:1958 3rd Qu.:68.29
     Max. :116.90 Max. :554.9 Max. :480.6 Max. :359.4 Max. :130.1 Max.
     :1962 Max. :70.55
    ```

3. Let's view the first six rows and last six rows of data by executing the following command:

```
> head(longley)
GNP.deflator GNP Unemployed Armed.Forces Population Year Employed

1947 83.0 234.289 235.6 159.0 107.608 1947 60.323
1948 88.5 259.426 232.5 145.6 108.632 1948 61.122
1949 88.2 258.054 368.2 161.6 109.773 1949 60.171
1950 89.5 284.599 335.1 165.0 110.929 1950 61.187
1951 96.2 328.975 209.9 309.9 112.075 1951 63.221
1952 98.1 346.999 193.2 359.4 113.270 1952 63.639


> tail(longley)

GNP.deflator GNP Unemployed Armed.Forces Population Year Employed

1957 108.4 442.769 293.6 279.8 120.445 1957 68.169
1958 110.8 444.546 468.1 263.7 121.950 1958 66.513
1959 112.6 482.704 381.3 255.2 123.366 1959 68.655
1960 114.2 502.601 393.1 251.4 125.368 1960 69.564
1961 115.7 518.173 480.6 257.2 127.852 1961 69.331
1962 116.9 554.894 400.7 282.7 130.081 1962 70.551
```

4. Renaming the columns as required is also equally important. The attributes of GNP Deflator and Armed Forces should be renamed properly as follows:

```
> View(longley)
> names(longley)[1]<-"GNP Deflator"
> names(longley)[4]<-"Armed Forces"
```

From here, we get the following output:

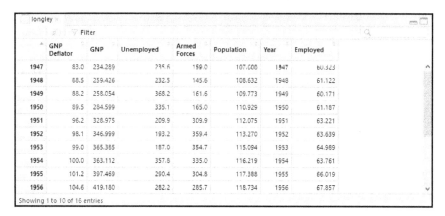

	GNP Deflator	GNP	Unemployed	Armed Forces	Population	Year	Employed
1947	83.0	234.289	235.6	159.0	107.608	1947	60.323
1948	88.5	259.426	232.5	145.6	108.632	1948	61.122
1949	88.2	258.054	368.2	161.6	109.773	1949	60.171
1950	89.5	284.599	335.1	165.0	110.929	1950	61.187
1951	96.2	328.975	209.9	309.9	112.075	1951	63.221
1952	98.1	346.999	193.2	359.4	113.270	1952	63.639
1953	99.0	365.385	187.0	354.7	115.094	1953	64.989
1954	100.0	363.112	357.8	335.0	116.219	1954	63.761
1955	101.2	397.469	290.4	304.8	117.388	1955	66.019
1956	104.6	419.180	282.2	285.7	118.734	1956	67.857

Showing 1 to 10 of 16 entries

Mapping and understanding the structure

This section involves understanding the depth of each and every attribute that is considered to be important for the previously mentioned dataset.

The following steps are used to map the underlying structure of our dataset:

1. Try to get a feel for the data as per the attribute structure:

   ```
   > class(longley)
   [1] "data.frame"
   ```

   The output shows that the dataset includes a tabular format of rows and columns that is well defined in dimensions.

2. Check the dimensions of the dataset:

   ```
   > dim(longley)
   [1] 16 7
   ```

   This means that the dataset is comprised of 858 rows and 36 columns. The column structure is as discussed in the first section.

3. View the column names of the dataset to check whether they match the records included in the Excel file:

   ```
   > colnames(longley)
   [1] "GNP Deflator" "GNP" "Unemployed" "Armed Forces" "Population"

   [6] "Year" "Employed"
   ```

4. Check the structure of our `longley` multivariate dataset by executing the following command:

   ```
   > str(longley)
   'data.frame': 16 obs. of 7 variables:

   $ GNP Deflator: num 83 88.5 88.2 89.5 96.2 ...
   $ GNP : num 234 259 258 285 329 ...
   $ Unemployed : num 236 232 368 335 210 ...
   $ Armed Forces: num 159 146 162 165 310 ...
   $ Population : num 108 109 110 111 112 ...
   $ Year : int 1947 1948 1949 1950 1951 1952 1953 1954 1955 1956 ...
   $ Employed : num 60.3 61.1 60.2 61.2 63.2 ...
   ```

The structure depicts the data type of each column and the values associated with it in numerical or decimal format.

5. Check the structure using the `dplyr` package:

```
> glimpse(longley)
Observations: 16

Variables: 7

$ `GNP Deflator` <dbl> 83.0, 88.5, 88.2, 89.5, 96.2, 98.1, 99.0,
100.0, 101.2, 104...

$ GNP <dbl> 234.289, 259.426, 258.054, 284.599, 328.975, 346.999,
365.3...

$ Unemployed <dbl> 235.6, 232.5, 368.2, 335.1, 209.9, 193.2, 187.0,
357.8, 290...

$ `Armed Forces` <dbl> 159.0, 145.6, 161.6, 165.0, 309.9, 359.4,
354.7, 335.0, 304...

$ Population <dbl> 107.608, 108.632, 109.773, 110.929, 112.075,
113.270, 115.0...

$ Year <int> 1947, 1948, 1949, 1950, 1951, 1952, 1953, 1954, 1955,
1956,...

$ Employed <dbl> 60.323, 61.122, 60.171, 61.187, 63.221, 63.639,
64.989, 63....
```

The `glimpse()` function makes it possible to have a look at each and every column of the data frame. It is similar to the `str()` function, the only difference being that it displays more data than the `str()` function, which is normally used to get the structure of the data.

6. Plot the important parameters of our data frame, which focuses on calculating the rate of unemployment with respect to the parameter of GNP:

```
> plot(longley$GNP, longley$Unemployed, main = "Rate of
Unemployment with GNP", xlab = "GNP", ylab = "Unemployed")
```

This gives us the following output:

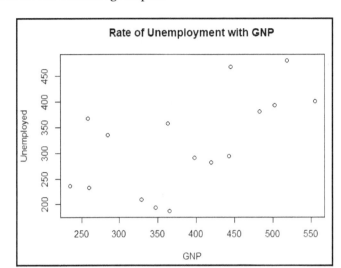

Hypothesis test

This section is all about hypothesis testing in R. This testing is merely an assumption made by the researcher about the population of data collected in relation to any experiment. As a first step, we will introduce the statistical hypothesis in R and later, we will cover the decision error in R, the one-and two-sample t-test, the u-test, correlation and covariance in R, and so on.

t-test in R

This is also referred to as the student's t-test, which is a method for comparing two samples. It can usually be implemented to determine whether the samples are proper or different. This is considered a parametric test, and the data should be distributed normally.

R can handle the various versions of the t-test using the t.test() command.

The following command is used for our longley economic dataset to check the unemployment rate with respect to GNP:

```
> t.test(longley$GNP, longley$Unemployed)
Welch Two Sample t-test
```

```
data: longley$GNP and longley$Unemployed

t = 2.0045, df = 29.886, p-value = 0.05415

alternative hypothesis: true difference in means is not equal to 0

95 percent confidence interval:

-1.297804 138.032179

sample estimates:

mean of x mean of y

387.6984 319.3313
```

The t.test() command is generally used to compare two vectors of numerical values. The vectors can be specified in a variety of ways, depending on how your data objects are set out.

Directional hypothesis in R

In this hypothesis testing, you can only specify a direction to the dataset mentioned previously. Here, we will use the same function with the alternative equal to (=) instruction to switch the emphasis from a two-sided test (the default) to a one-sided test. The choices that we can have are two.sided, less, or greater, and the choice can be abbreviated, as shown in the following command:

```
> t.test(longley$GNP, mu = 5, alternative = 'two.sided')
One Sample t-test
data: longley$GNP
t = 15.401, df = 15, p-value = 1.337e-10

alternative hypothesis: true mean is not equal to 5
95 percent confidence interval:

334.7346 440.6623

sample estimates:
mean of x
387.6984

> t.test(longley$Unemployed, mu = 5, alternative = 'two.sided')
One Sample t-test
data: longley$Unemployed
```

```
t = 13.455, df = 15, p-value = 8.912e-10

alternative hypothesis: true mean is not equal to 5
95 percent confidence interval:
269.5372 369.1253
sample estimates:
mean of x
319.3313
```

It is clear that the values generated include sample estimates. We can also see that the mean of x is calculated as 319.33 for the unemployment rate as per the economic regression dataset. This also means that the error generated is quite low in comparison to other attributes.

Parsimonious model

Parsimonious models are simple models with great explanatory predictive power. They usually explain data with a minimum number of parameters or predictor variables. MoEClust is the required R package, which fits finite Gaussian Mixtures of Experts models using a range of parsimonious covariance with the help of EM/CEM algorithms.

The following steps need to be carried out to perform Parsimonious data analysis:

1. Install the following requisite package that is needed to create a parsimonious model of our longley economic dataset:

```
> install.packages('devtools')
Installing package into 'C:/Users/Radhika/Documents/R/win-
library/3.5'
(as 'lib' is unspecified)
trying URL
'https://cran.rstudio.com/bin/windows/contrib/3.5/devtools_2.0.2.zi
p'
Content type 'application/zip' length 383720 bytes (374 KB)
downloaded 374 KB
package 'devtools' successfully unpacked and MD5 sums checked
The downloaded binary packages are in
 C:\Users\Radhika\AppData\Local\Temp\Rtmpc1oW5p\downloaded_packages

> install.packages('MoEClust')
Installing package into 'C:/Users/Radhika/Documents/R/win-
library/3.5'
(as 'lib' is unspecified)
trying URL
'https://cran.rstudio.com/bin/windows/contrib/3.5/MoEClust_1.2.1.zi
```

```
p'
Content type 'application/zip' length 759555 bytes (741 KB)
downloaded 741 KB
package 'MoEClust' successfully unpacked and MD5 sums checked
The downloaded binary packages are in
 C:\Users\Radhika\AppData\Local\Temp\Rtmpc1oW5p\downloaded_packages
> library(MoEClust)

___ ___ _____ _____ _ _
| \/ | | ___/ _ \ | | | Gaussian Parsimonious
| . . |  __ | |_ | / \/ |_ _ ___| |_ Clustering Models
| |\/| |/ _ \| __|| | | | | | | / __| __| with Covariates
| | | | (_) | | |__| \__/\ | | |_| \__ \ | |_
\_| |_/\___/\____/ \____/_|\__,_|___/\__| version 1.2.1

Type '?MoEClust' to see a brief guide to how to use this R package.
Type 'citation("MoEClust")' for citing the package in publications.
Type 'MoE_news()' to see new features recent changes and bug fixes.

Warning message:
package 'MoEClust' was built under R version 3.5.3
```

This package helps in clustering the data as per the required value analysis.

2. Create separate data variables with the parameters of the `longley` economic regression dataset, which includes various parameters of economic growth:

```
> GNP<-longley[,2]
> Unemployed<-longley[,3]
> Population<-longley[,5]
> dim(longley)
[1] 16  7
```

3. For models with covariates in the gating network, or models with equal mixing proportions, there is no need to fit single component models. We will focus on the GNP parameter as follows:

```
> m1 <- MoE_clust(GNP, G=0:2, verbose=FALSE)
> m2 <- MoE_clust(GNP, G=2, verbose=FALSE)
> m3 <- MoE_clust(GNP, G=2:16, verbose=FALSE)
> m1
Call: MoE_clust(data = GNP, G = 0:2, verbose = FALSE)
Best Model (according to BIC): univariate, equal variance (E), with
only a noise component
Equal Mixing Proportions
Hypervolume of Noise Component: 320.605
BIC = -187.419 | ICL = -187.419 | AIC = -186.647
No covariates
> m2
```

```
Call: MoE_clust(data = GNP, G = 2, verbose = FALSE)
Best Model (according to BIC): univariate, equal variance (E), with
2 components
BIC = -200.976 | ICL = -204.163 | AIC = -197.886
No covariates
> m3
Call: MoE_clust(data = GNP, G = 2:15, verbose = FALSE)
Best Model (according to BIC): univariate, equal variance (E), with
2 components
BIC = -200.976 | ICL = -204.163 | AIC = -197.886
No covariates
```

4. This step involves a comparison of the data values and the covariates required:

```
> comp <- MoE_compare(m1, m2, m3)
> comp
--------------------------------------------------------------------
-----------
Comparison of Gaussian Parsimonious Clustering Models with
Covariates
Data: GNP
--------------------------------------------------------------------
-----------

rank MoENames modelNames G df iters bic icl aic loglik gating
expert
 1 m1 E 0 1 1 -187.419 -187.419 -186.647 -92.323 None None
 2 m1 E 1 2 1 -197.09 -197.09 -195.545 -95.772 None None
 3 m1 E 2 4 9 -200.976 -204.163 -197.886 -94.943 None None
equalPro noise
FALSE NULL
TRUE FALSE
FALSE FALSE
```

5. Convert the `MoEClust` class to the `Mclust` class in order to visualize the results with respect to the classification options as follows:

```
> (mod <- as.Mclust(comp$optimal))
'Mclust' model object: single noise component

Available components:
 [1] "call" "data" "modelName" "n"
 [5] "d" "G" "BIC" "bic"
 [9] "loglik" "df" "hypvol" "parameters"
[13] "z" "classification" "uncertainty"

> plot(mod, what="classification")
```

The plot created is as follows:

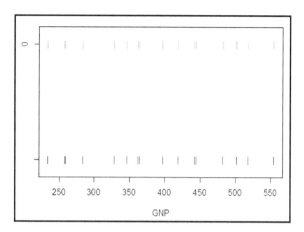

Levene's test

Levene's test checks are used to understand homogeneous variances in attributes in relation to the data frame mentioned and the null hypothesis test is used to verify the fact that all variances are equal. A resulting p-value that is calculated as being under 0.05 using this test means that variances are not equal and further parametric analysis tests, such as ANOVA, are not considered appropriate.

 This test is usually preferred with normally distributed data, but it can also tolerate a comparatively low deviation from normality.

The corresponding function in R is as follows:

```
leveneTest(dataset~groups, data=dataframe)
```

Here, the parameters refer to the following:

- `dataset`: The vector containing the numerical data
- `groups`: The vector that contains the names or labels of the groups that need to be compared

`data=` is followed by the name of the whole data frame containing datasets and groups.

The `leveneTest()` function is found in the pre-installed package called `car` in R. The following steps are executed for performing Levene's test on the `longley` dataset:

1. Include the `car` library in your specified workspace:

```
> library(car)
Loading required package: carData

Attaching package: 'car'

The following object is masked from 'package:dplyr':

recode

The following object is masked from 'package:arules':

recode

Warning message:
package 'car' was built under R version 3.5.1
```

2. Perform Levene's test for GNP and unemployment rate:

```
> leveneTest(longley$GNP, longley$Unemployed)
Levene's Test for Homogeneity of Variance (center = median)
      Df F value Pr(>F)
group 15
       0
```

Data visualization

In this section, we will focus on creating the scatter plots for the given dataset. Creating scatter plots involves new feature analysis with the help of the ggplot2 package:

1. Include the library in the specified workspace. This involves execution of the following set of commands:

```
> library('ggplot2')

Attaching package: 'ggplot2'

The following object is masked _by_ '.GlobalEnv':

mpg

Warning message:
package 'ggplot2' was built under R version 3.5.3
> library(readr)
```

2. Create the parameters in a systematic way that will help to resize the plots in the way we want:

```
> options(repr.plot.width = 6, repr.plot.height = 6)
```

3. This step involves loading the data in our R workspace. Basically, with this step, we will convert the CSV file into a systematic dataset:

```
> class(longley)
[1] "data.frame"
"
```

4. Once the dataset is created, we can view it. This can also be achieved by looking at the first five rows of the dataset:

```
> View(longley)
> head(longley)
 GNP Deflator GNP Unemployed Armed Forces Population Year Employed
1947 83.0 234.289 235.6 159.0 107.608 1947 60.323
1948 88.5 259.426 232.5 145.6 108.632 1948 61.122
1949 88.2 258.054 368.2 161.6 109.773 1949 60.171
1950 89.5 284.599 335.1 165.0 110.929 1950 61.187
1951 96.2 328.975 209.9 309.9 112.075 1951 63.221
1952 98.1 346.999 193.2 359.4 113.270 1952 63.639
```

The View() function will display the systematic creation of the dataset that we have achieved successfully with the previous set of commands, as can be seen in the following screenshot:

	GNP Deflator	GNP	Unemployed	Armed Forces	Population	Year	Employed
1947	83.0	234.289	235.6	159.0	107.608	1947	60.323
1948	88.5	259.426	232.5	145.6	108.632	1948	61.122
1949	88.2	258.054	368.2	161.6	109.773	1949	60.171
1950	89.5	284.599	335.1	165.0	110.929	1950	61.187
1951	96.2	328.975	209.9	309.9	112.075	1951	63.221
1952	98.1	346.999	193.2	359.4	113.270	1952	63.639
1953	99.0	365.385	187.0	354.7	115.094	1953	64.989
1954	100.0	363.112	357.8	335.0	116.219	1954	63.761
1955	101.2	397.469	290.4	304.8	117.388	1955	66.019
1956	104.6	419.180	282.2	285.7	118.734	1956	67.857

Showing 1 to 10 of 16 entries

5. With the help of the summary() function, we could also check and analyze the statistic summary of the longley economic regression data:

```
> summary(longley)
 GNP Deflator GNP Unemployed Armed Forces Population
 Min. : 83.00 Min. :234.3 Min. :187.0 Min. :145.6 Min. :107.6
 1st Qu.: 94.53 1st Qu.:317.9 1st Qu.:234.8 1st Qu.:229.8 1st
Qu.:111.8
 Median :100.60 Median :381.4 Median :314.4 Median :271.8 Median
:116.8
 Mean :101.68 Mean :387.7 Mean :319.3 Mean :260.7 Mean :117.4
 3rd Qu.:111.25 3rd Qu.:454.1 3rd Qu.:384.2 3rd Qu.:306.1 3rd
Qu.:122.3
 Max. :116.90 Max. :554.9 Max. :480.6 Max. :359.4 Max. :130.1
 Year Employed
 Min. :1947 Min. :60.17
 1st Qu.:1951 1st Qu.:62.71
 Median :1954 Median :65.50
 Mean :1954 Mean :65.32
 3rd Qu.:1958 3rd Qu.:68.29
 Max. :1962 Max. :70.55
```

6. We can check the unemployment rate with respect to GNP. This can be achieved with the help of scatter plot creation, which is executed with the help of the following command:

```
> ggplot(data=longley,aes(x=longley$GNP, y=longley$Unemployed)) +
geom_point() + theme_minimal()
> ggplot(data=longley,aes(x=longley$`GNP Deflator`,
y=longley$Unemployed)) + geom_point() + theme_minimal()
```

This gives us the following output plot for `longley$GNP`:

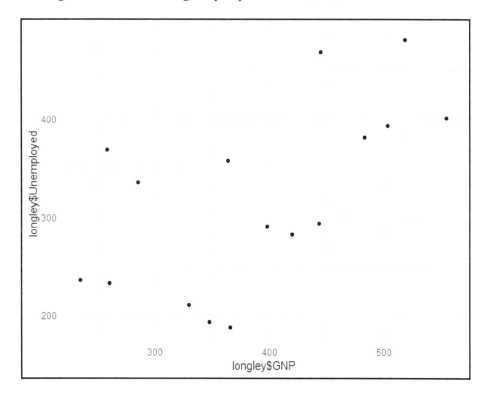

This gives us the following output plot for `longley$`GNP Deflator`:

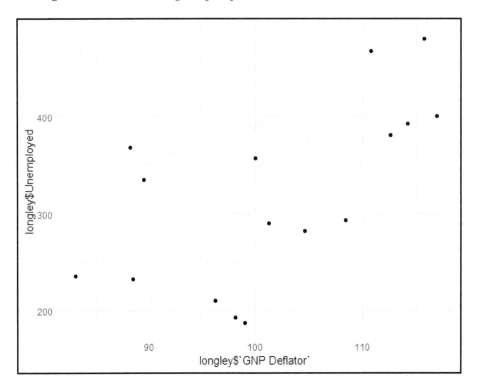

7. Create the matrix scatter plots from the list of attributes by executing the following command:

```
> pairs(longley[,1:4], pch = 19)
> pairs(longley[,5:7], pch = 19)
```

The first output plot is as follows:

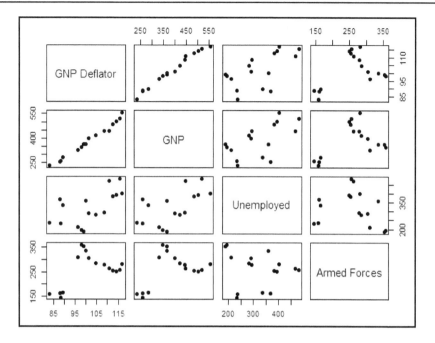

The second output plot is as follows:

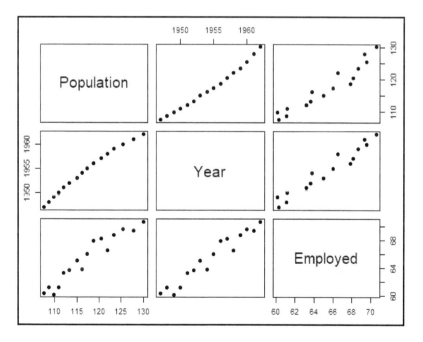

Stepwise linear regression is considered an important method that makes use of linear regression to discover attribute subsets in the dataset that result in the best performing model. It is a stepwise approach or algorithm where each iteration of the method makes a change to the set of attributes and creates a model to evaluate the performance of the set:

```
> base<-lm(Employed ~., longley)
> summary(base)

Call:
lm(formula = Employed ~ ., data = longley)

Residuals:
 Min 1Q Median 3Q Max
-0.41011 -0.15767 -0.02816 0.10155 0.45539

Coefficients:
 Estimate Std. Error t value Pr(>|t|)
(Intercept) -3.482e+03 8.904e+02 -3.911 0.003560 **
`GNP Deflator` 1.506e-02 8.492e-02 0.177 0.863141
GNP -3.582e-02 3.349e-02 -1.070 0.312681
Unemployed -2.020e-02 4.884e-03 -4.136 0.002535 **
`Armed Forces` -1.033e-02 2.143e-03 -4.822 0.000944 ***
Population -5.110e-02 2.261e-01 -0.226 0.826212
Year 1.829e+00 4.555e-01 4.016 0.003037 **
---
Signif. codes: 0 '***' 0.001 '**' 0.01 '*' 0.05 '.' 0.1 ' ' 1

Residual standard error: 0.3049 on 9 degrees of freedom
Multiple R-squared: 0.9955, Adjusted R-squared: 0.9925
F-statistic: 330.3 on 6 and 9 DF, p-value: 4.984e-10

> slrFit<-step(base)
Start: AIC=-33.22
Employed ~ `GNP Deflator` + GNP + Unemployed + `Armed Forces` +
 Population + Year

Df Sum of Sq RSS AIC
- `GNP Deflator` 1 0.00292 0.83935 -35.163
- Population 1 0.00475 0.84117 -35.129
- GNP 1 0.10631 0.94273 -33.305
<none> 0.83642 -33.219
- Year 1 1.49881 2.33524 -18.792
- Unemployed 1 1.59014 2.42656 -18.178
- `Armed Forces` 1 2.16091 2.99733 -14.798

Step: AIC=-35.16
Employed ~ GNP + Unemployed + `Armed Forces` + Population + Year
```

```
Df Sum of Sq RSS AIC
- Population 1 0.01933 0.8587 -36.799
<none> 0.8393 -35.163
- GNP 1 0.14637 0.9857 -34.592
- Year 1 1.52725 2.3666 -20.578
- Unemployed 1 2.18989 3.0292 -16.628
- `Armed Forces` 1 2.39752 3.2369 -15.568

Step: AIC=-36.8
Employed ~ GNP + Unemployed + `Armed Forces` + Year

Df Sum of Sq RSS AIC
<none> 0.8587 -36.799
- GNP 1 0.4647 1.3234 -31.879
- Year 1 1.8980 2.7567 -20.137
- `Armed Forces` 1 2.3806 3.2393 -17.556
- Unemployed 1 4.0491 4.9077 -10.908

> #Make predictions
> slrPredictions<-predict(slrFit, longley)
> slrMSE<-mean((longley$Employed - slrPredictions)^2)
> print(slrMSE)
[1] 0.05366753
> plot(slrPredictions)
```

The linear regression plot generated is shown as follows:

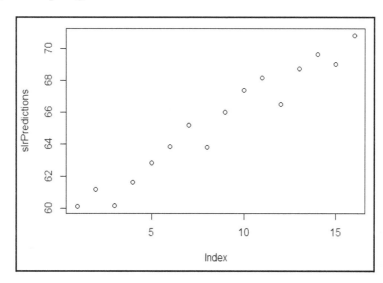

Let's focus on **Principal Component Regression** (**PCR**) with this economic dataset, which is considered the most suitable example of regression.

Principal Component Regression

This model helps to create a linear regression model using the outputs of a **Principal Component Analysis (PCA)** to estimate the coefficients of the model. PCR is useful when the data has highly correlated predictors:

```
> pcrFit<-pcr(Employed ~ ., data = longley, valdiation = "cv")
> summary(pcrFit)
Data: X dimension: 16 6
 Y dimension: 16 1
Fit method: svdpc
Number of components considered: 6
TRAINING: % variance explained
 1 comps 2 comps 3 comps 4 comps 5 comps 6 comps
X 64.96 94.90 99.99 100.00 100.00 100.00
Employed 78.42 89.73 98.51 98.56 98.83 99.55
> #Make predictions
> pcrPredictions<-predict(pcrFit, longley, ncomp = 6)
> #Include accuracy parameter
> pcrMSE<-mean((longley$Employed - pcrPredictions)^2)
> print(pcrMSE)
[1] 0.0522765
> plot(pcrMSE)
```

This gives us the following output plot:

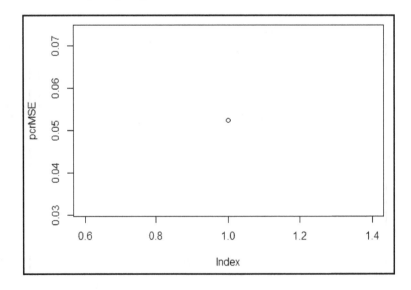

Partial Least Squares Regression

Partial Least Squares Regression (**PLSR**) creates a linear model of the data in a transformed projection of a problem space. Like PCR, PLSR is appropriate for data with highly correlated predictors, shown as follows:

```
> plsFit<-plsr(Employed ~., data = longley, validation = "CV")
> #summarise the fit model
> summary(plsFit)
Data: X dimension: 16 6
 Y dimension: 16 1
Fit method: kernelpls
Number of components considered: 6

VALIDATION: RMSEP
Cross-validated using 10 random segments.
 (Intercept) 1 comps 2 comps 3 comps 4 comps 5 comps 6 comps
CV 3.627 1.415 1.063 0.5404 0.6336 0.4696 0.4197
adjCV 3.627 1.397 1.052 0.5324 0.6168 0.4644 0.4076

TRAINING: % variance explained
 1 comps 2 comps 3 comps 4 comps 5 comps 6 comps
X 63.88 93.35 99.99 100.00 100.00 100.00
Employed 87.91 93.70 98.51 98.65 99.16 99.55
> #make predictions
> plsPredictions<-predict(plsFit, longley, ncomp = 6)
> plsMSE<-mean((longley$Employed - plsPredictions)^2)
> print(plsMSE)
[1] 0.0522765
> plot(plsMSE)
```

This gives us the following output plot:

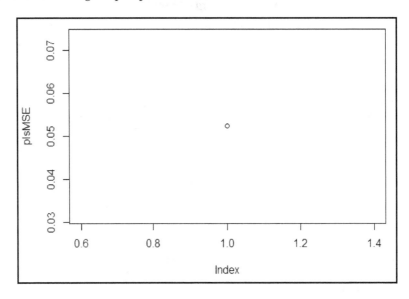

Summary

In this chapter, we have focused on the implementation of all libraries of a multivariate dataset that is strongly linked to time series creation. The best illustration is to check the parameters of Longley's Economic Regression Data and parsimonious models for creating accuracy fit models. We have listed some of the various packages that are available for reading in various kinds of attributes within the dataset mentioned previously in R. There are lots of different options and even the options we have listed have a wide functionality that we are going to cover and use as we go further into this book.

In the next chapter, we will introduce a multi-factor dataset and explain how to use exploratory data analysis techniques to analyze this data.

3
Section 3: Multifactor, Optimization, and Regression Data Problems

Here, we introduce a dataset from the regression problem category and a multifactor dataset to use exploratory data analysis techniques to analyze data.

The following chapters will be covered in this section:

Chapter 9, *Multifactor Datasets*

Chapter 10, *Handling Optimization and Regression Data Problems*

9
Multi-Factor Datasets

This chapter will introduce a multi-factor dataset and explain how to use exploratory data analysis techniques to analyze this data. In previous chapters, we focused on univariate and multivariate datasets. Univariate and multivariate datasets represent two patterns to statistical analysis. Univariate analysis involves the analysis of a single variable, while multivariate analysis involves the analysis of two or more variables.
Most multivariate analysis involves implementation of dependent variable and multiple independent variables. Multiple factor datasets simultaneously analyze several tables of variables to obtain results. In this chapter, we will first learn to read and tidy the data, after which we will learn to map and understand the underlying structure of the dataset and identify the important variables. We will then create a list of outliers or other anomalies with Grubbs' test and then uncover a parsimonious model. We will also learn and use the exploratory data analysis techniques of DOE scatter plot, DOE mean plot, DOE standard deviation plot, and contour plot. We will also explore and analyze the auto MPG dataset from UCI.

The following topics will be covered in this chapter:

- Introducing and reading in the data
- Cleaning and tidying up the data
- Mapping and understanding the underlying structure of the dataset and identifying the most important variables
- Testing assumptions and hypotheses, estimating parameters, and figuring the margins of error
- Creating a list of outliers or other anomalies with Grubbs' test
- Uncovering a parsimonious model
- Running multi-factor variance analysis
- Exploring the dataset graphically using DOE scatter plot, DOE mean plot, DOE standard deviation plot, and contour plot
- Summarizing our findings

Technical requirements

You should have hands-on experience or knowledge of the following points before getting started with this chapter:

- R programming language
- RStudio
- R packages
  (including `readr`, `readxl`, `jsonlite`, `httr`, `rvest`, `DBI`, `dplyr`, `stringr`, `forc ats`, `lubridate`, `hms`, `blob`, `ggplot2`, and `knitr`)

Introducing and reading the dataset

This dataset is provided in the `StatLib` library, predicting the `mpg` attribute where eight of the original instances were removed because they had unknown values for the `mpg` attribute. The original dataset is available in the `auto-mpg.data-original` file on the UCI website and you can refer to it using the following link: `https://archive.ics.uci.edu/ ml/datasets/auto+mpg`.

We will be using data available at the following link: `https://github.com/ PacktPublishing/Hands-On-Exploratory-Data-Analysis-with-R/tree/master/ch09`.

As mentioned on their website, *The data concerns city-cycle fuel consumption in miles per gallon, to be predicted in terms of three multivalued discrete, and five continuous, attributes.*

This section is all about understanding the dataset and its attributes. We will carry out the following steps as we did in the previous chapters to understand the attribute structure, or rather, metadata information pertaining to the dataset:

1. Import the dataset from the URL in the R workspace indicated as follows:

```
> library(readr)
> Autompg <- read.csv("auto-mpg.csv")

> Autompg

> View(Autompg)
```

This gives us the following dataset:

	mpg	cylinders	displacement	horsepower	weight	acceleration	model.year	origin	car.name
1	18	8	307.0	130	3504	12.0	70	1	chevrolet chevelle malibu
2	15	8	350.0	165	3693	11.5	70	1	buick skylark 320
3	18	8	318.0	150	3436	11.0	70	1	plymouth satellite
4	16	8	304.0	150	3433	12.0	70	1	amc rebel sst
5	17	8	302.0	140	3449	10.5	70	1	ford torino
6	15	8	429.0	198	4341	10.0	70	1	ford galaxie 500
7	14	8	454.0	220	4354	9.0	70	1	chevrolet impala
8	14	8	440.0	215	4312	8.5	70	1	plymouth fury iii
9	14	8	455.0	225	4425	10.0	70	1	pontiac catalina
10	15	8	390.0	190	3850	8.5	70	1	amc ambassador dpl
11	15	8	383.0	170	3563	10.0	70	1	dodge challenger se
12	14	8	340.0	160	3609	8.0	70	1	plymouth 'cuda 340

Showing 1 to 12 of 398 entries

2. We now need to focus on the structure of the data frame with the required function, as shown in the following code:

```
> str(Autompg)
'data.frame': 398 obs. of 9 variables:

$ mpg : num 18 15 18 16 17 15 14 14 14 15 ...

$ cylinders : int 8 8 8 8 8 8 8 8 8 8 ...

$ displacement: num 307 350 318 304 302 429 454 440 455 390 ...

$ horsepower : Factor w/ 94 levels "?","100","102",..: 17 35 29 29
24 42 47 46 48 40 ...

$ weight : int 3504 3693 3436 3433 3449 4341 4354 4312 4425 3850
...

$ acceleration: num 12 11.5 11 12 10.5 10 9 8.5 10 8.5 ...

$ model.year : int 70 70 70 70 70 70 70 70 70 70 ...

$ origin : int 1 1 1 1 1 1 1 1 1 1 ...

$ car.name : Factor w/ 305 levels "amc ambassador brougham",..: 50
37 232 15 162 142 55 224 242 2 ...
```

Let's cover the attribute names and their description from our dataset, or rather our data frame, as outlined in the following table:

Attribute	Description
mpg	Numeric continuous value of cars.
cylinders	The multi-valued discrete value of the cylinders.
displacement	Automobile displacement value.
weight	Automobile weight. This is a continuous variable.
acceleration	Automobile acceleration. This is a continuous variable.
model.year	This is a multi-valued discrete variable, that defines the model of the year.
origin	This is a multi-valued discrete variable, that defines the origin of the model.
car.name	This is a string value specifying the name of the car.

Cleaning the dataset

Data cleaning is the process of converting the raw data into a specific format that includes consistent data designed in a simpler manner. R includes a set of comprehensive tools, that are designed specially to clean the data in an effective manner. We will try to focus on cleaning the dataset here in a specific way and will carry out the following steps to this end:

1. Include the libraries that are needed to clean and tidy up the dataset as follows:

```
> library(dplyr)
> library(tidyr)
```

2. Analyze the summary of our dataset as shown in the following code. This will help us to focus on which attributes are important:

```
> summary(Autompg)
mpg cylinders displacement horsepower weight acceleration
Min. : 9.00 Min. :3.000 Min. : 68.0 150 : 22 Min. :1613 Min. : 8.00
1st Qu.:17.50 1st Qu.:4.000 1st Qu.:104.2 90 : 20 1st Qu.:2224 1st
Qu.:13.82
Median :23.00 Median :4.000 Median :148.5 88 : 19 Median :2804
Median :15.50
Mean :23.51 Mean :5.455 Mean :193.4 110 : 18 Mean :2970 Mean :15.57
3rd Qu.:29.00 3rd Qu.:8.000 3rd Qu.:262.0 100 : 17 3rd Qu.:3608 3rd
Qu.:17.18
Max. :46.60 Max. :8.000 Max. :455.0 75 : 14 Max. :5140 Max. :24.80
(Other) :288
model.year origin car.name
```

```
Min. :70.00 Min. :1.000 ford pinto : 6
1st Qu.:73.00 1st Qu.:1.000 amc matador : 5
Median :76.00 Median :1.000 ford maverick : 5
Mean :76.01 Mean :1.573 toyota corolla: 5
3rd Qu.:79.00 3rd Qu.:2.000 amc gremlin : 4
Max. :82.00 Max. :3.000 amc hornet : 4
(Other) :369
```

3. Let's view the first six columns and last six columns of data by executing the following command:

```
>  head(Autompg)
 mpg cylinders displacement horsepower weight acceleration
model.year origin
1 18 8 307 130 3504 12.0 70 1
2 15 8 350 165 3693 11.5 70 1
3 18 8 318 150 3436 11.0 70 1
4 16 8 304 150 3433 12.0 70 1
5 17 8 302 140 3449 10.5 70 1
6 15 8 429 198 4341 10.0 70 1
car.name
1 chevrolet chevelle malibu
2 buick skylark 320
3 plymouth satellite
4 amc rebel sst
5 ford torino
6 ford galaxie 500

> tail(Autompg)

mpg cylinders displacement horsepower weight acceleration
model.year origin car.name

393 27 4 151 90 2950 17.3 82 1 chevrolet camaro

394 27 4 140 86 2790 15.6 82 1 ford mustang gl

395 44 4 97 52 2130 24.6 82 2 vw pickup

396 32 4 135 84 2295 11.6 82 1 dodge rampage

397 28 4 120 79 2625 18.6 82 1 ford ranger

398 31 4 119 82 2720 19.4 82 1 chevy s-10
```

4. Renaming the columns as required is also equally important. Here, we can rename certain columns to suit our needs:

```
> > names(Autompg)[9]<-"CarName"
> View(Autompg)
```

This gives us the following output:

	mpg	cylinders	displacement	horsepower	weight	acceleration	model.year	origin	CarName
1	18	8	307.0	130	3504	12.0	70	1	chevrolet chevelle malibu
2	15	8	350.0	165	3693	11.5	70	1	buick skylark 320
3	18	8	318.0	150	3436	11.0	70	1	plymouth satellite
4	16	8	304.0	150	3433	12.0	70	1	amc rebel sst
5	17	8	302.0	140	3449	10.5	70	1	ford torino
6	15	8	429.0	198	4341	10.0	70	1	ford galaxie 500
7	14	8	454.0	220	4354	9.0	70	1	chevrolet impala
8	14	8	440.0	215	4312	8.5	70	1	plymouth fury iii
9	14	8	455.0	225	4425	10.0	70	1	pontiac catalina
10	15	8	390.0	190	3850	8.5	70	1	amc ambassador dpl

5. Based on the results of the preceding `str(cars)` function, it is observed that there are several issues with how the `read.csv` function is imported. The data needs to be cleaned before proceeding with an in-depth analysis:

```
> Autompg$cylinders = Autompg$cylinders %>%
+   factor(labels = sort(unique(Autompg$cylinders)))
> Autompg$horsepower =
as.numeric(levels(Autompg$horsepower))[Autompg$horsepower]
> View(Autompg)
```

This gives us the following output:

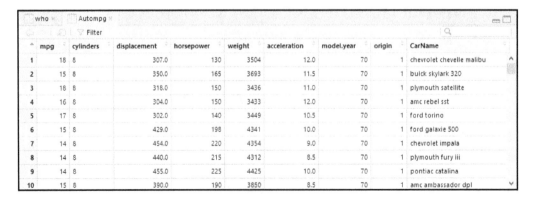

	mpg	cylinders	displacement	horsepower	weight	acceleration	model.year	origin	CarName
1	18	8	307.0	130	3504	12.0	70	1	chevrolet chevelle malibu
2	15	8	350.0	165	3693	11.5	70	1	buick skylark 320
3	18	8	318.0	150	3436	11.0	70	1	plymouth satellite
4	16	8	304.0	150	3433	12.0	70	1	amc rebel sst
5	17	8	302.0	140	3449	10.5	70	1	ford torino
6	15	8	429.0	198	4341	10.0	70	1	ford galaxie 500
7	14	8	454.0	220	4354	9.0	70	1	chevrolet impala
8	14	8	440.0	215	4312	8.5	70	1	plymouth fury iii
9	14	8	455.0	225	4425	10.0	70	1	pontiac catalina
10	15	8	390.0	190	3850	8.5	70	1	amc ambassador dpl

Mapping and understanding data structure

This section involves understanding each and every attribute in depth, which is considered to be important for the dataset indicated:

1. Try to get a feel for the data as per the attribute structure by executing the following command:

   ```
   > class(Autompg)
    [1] "data.frame"
   ```

   The output shows that the dataset is merely a tabular format of a data frame.

2. Check the dimensions of the dataset by executing the following command:

   ```
   > dim(Autompg)
   [1] 398 9
   ```

   This means that the dataset comprises 398 rows and 9 columns. The column structure is discussed in the first section.

3. View the column names of the dataset as follows to establish whether they correspond to the records included in the Excel file:

   ```
   > colnames(Autompg)
    [1] "mpg" "cylinders" "displacement" "horsepower" "weight"
   "acceleration"
   [7] "model.year" "origin" "CarName"
   ```

4. Check the structure of the AutoMpg dataset by executing the following command:

   ```
   > str(Autompg)
   'data.frame': 398 obs. of 9 variables:
   $ mpg : num 18 15 18 16 17 15 14 14 14 15 ...
   $ cylinders : Factor w/ 5 levels "3","4","5","6",..: 5 5 5 5 5 5 5
   5 5 5 ...
   $ displacement: num 307 350 318 304 302 429 454 440 455 390 ...
   $ horsepower : num 130 165 150 150 140 198 220 215 225 190 ...
   $ weight : int 3504 3693 3436 3433 3449 4341 4354 4312 4425 3850
   ...
   $ acceleration: num 12 11.5 11 12 10.5 10 9 8.5 10 8.5 ...
   $ model.year : int 70 70 70 70 70 70 70 70 70 70 ...
   $ origin : int 1 1 1 1 1 1 1 1 1 1 ...
   $ CarName : Factor w/ 305 levels "amc ambassador brougham",..: 50
   37 232 15 162 142 55 224 242 2 ...
   ```

The preceding structure depicts the data type for each column and the values associated with it, such as numerical or decimal format.

5. Check the structure using the following `dplyr` package:

```
> glimpse(Autompg)
Observations: 398

Variables: 9

$ mpg <dbl> 18, 15, 18, 16, 17, 15, 14, 14, 14, 15, 15, 14, 15, 14,
24, 22, 18, 21, 27...

$ cylinders <fct> 8, 8, 8, 8, 8, 8, 8, 8, 8, 8, 8, 8, 8, 8, 4, 6,
6, 6, 4, 4, 4, 4, 4, 4, 6,...

$ displacement <dbl> 307, 350, 318, 304, 302, 429, 454, 440, 455,
390, 383, 340, 400, 455, 113,...

$ horsepower <dbl> 130, 165, 150, 150, 140, 198, 220, 215, 225,
190, 170, 160, 150, 225, 95, ...

$ weight <int> 3504, 3693, 3436, 3433, 3449, 4341, 4354, 4312,
4425, 3850, 3563, 3609, 37...

$ acceleration <dbl> 12.0, 11.5, 11.0, 12.0, 10.5, 10.0, 9.0, 8.5,
10.0, 8.5, 10.0, 8.0, 9.5, 1...

$ model.year <int> 70, 70, 70, 70, 70, 70, 70, 70, 70, 70, 70, 70,
70, 70, 70, 70, 70, 70, 70...

$ origin <int> 1, 1, 1, 1, 1, 1, 1, 1, 1, 1, 1, 1, 1, 1, 3, 1, 1,
1, 3, 2, 2, 2, 2, 1,...

$ CarName <fct> chevrolet chevelle malibu, buick skylark 320,
plymouth satellite, amc rebe...
```

The `glimpse()` function makes it possible to have a look at each and every column of the data frame. It is similar to `str()`, the only difference being that it displays more data than the `str()` function, which is normally used to obtain the structure of data.

6. Plot the important parameters of our data frame, which focuses on calculating the acceleration rate with respect to displacement (distance covered):

```
> plot(Autompg$displacement, Autompg$acceleration, main = "Rate of
acceleration", xlab = "Displacement", ylab = "Acceleration")
```

This gives us the following plot:

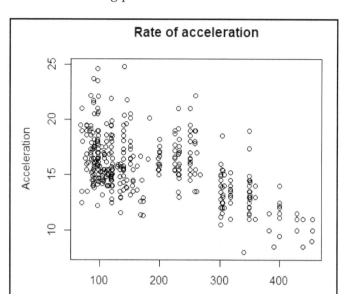

Hypothesis test

This section is all about hypothesis testing in R. This testing is merely an assumption made by the researcher about the population of data collected in relation to any experiment. As a first step, we will introduce the statistical hypothesis in R, and later, we will cover the decision error in R with a single t-test and directional hypothesis in R.

t-test in R

This is also referred to as the student's t-test, which is a method for comparing two samples. It can usually be implemented to determine whether the samples are proper or different. This is considered a parametric test, and the data should be distributed normally.

R can handle the various versions of t-test using the t.test() command.

The following command is used for our `Autompg` dataset to check the parameters of displacement, weight, and acceleration, which are regarded as crucial elements to perform the hypothesis test error analysis:

```
> > t.test(Autompg$displacement, Autompg$weight)
Welch Two Sample t-test
                data: Autompg$displacement and Autompg$weight
                t = -64.93, df = 409.03, p-value < 2.2e-16
                alternative hypothesis: true difference in means is not
equal to 0
                95 percent confidence interval:
                 -2861.073 -2692.924
                sample estimates:
                mean of x mean of y
                 193.4259 2970.4246
```

The `t.test()` command is generally used to compare two vectors of numerical values. The vectors can be specified in a variety of ways, depending on how your data objects are set out.

Directional hypothesis in R

In this hypothesis testing, you can only specify a direction to the dataset mentioned previously. Here, we will use the same function with the alternative equal to (=) instruction to switch the emphasis from a two-sided test (the default) to a one-sided test. The choices that we have are `two.sided`, `less`, or `greater`, and the choice can be abbreviated, as shown in the following command:

```
> t.test(Autompg$displacement, mu = 5, alternative = 'greater')

   One Sample t-test

data: Autompg$displacement
t = 36.052, df = 397, p-value < 2.2e-16
alternative hypothesis: true mean is greater than 5
95 percent confidence interval:
 184.8088 Inf
sample estimates:
mean of x
 193.4259


> t.test(Autompg$displacement, mu = 5, alternative = 'two.sided')

   One Sample t-test
```

```
data: Autompg$displacement
t = 36.052, df = 397, p-value < 2.2e-16
alternative hypothesis: true mean is not equal to 5
95 percent confidence interval:
 183.1507 203.7011
sample estimates:
mean of x
 193.4259
```

It is clear that the values generated include sample estimates, and the mean of x is calculated as 0.0641 for the displacement of each automobile. This also means that the error generated is considerably less in comparison to other attributes.

Grubbs test and checking outliers

In statistics, or particularly in R programming, an **outlier** is defined as an observation that is far removed from most of the other observations. Often, an outlier is present due to a measurement error.

The following script is used to detect the particular outliers for each and every attribute:

```
> outlierKD <- function(dt, var) {
+
        var_name <- eval(substitute(var),eval(dt))
        +
        na1 <- sum(is.na(var_name))
        +
        m1 <- mean(var_name, na.rm = T)
        +
        par(mfrow=c(2, 2), oma=c(0,0,3,0))
        +
        boxplot(var_name, main="With outliers")
        +
        hist(var_name, main="With outliers", xlab=NA, ylab=NA)
        +
        outlier <- boxplot.stats(var_name)$out
        +
        mo <- mean(outlier)
        +
        var_name <- ifelse(var_name %in% outlier, NA, var_name)
        +
        boxplot(var_name, main="Without outliers")
        +
        hist(var_name, main="Without outliers", xlab=NA, ylab=NA)
```

```
+
      title("Outlier Check", outer=TRUE)
+
      na2 <- sum(is.na(var_name))
+
      cat("Outliers identified:", na2 - na1, "n")
+
      cat("Proportion (%) of outliers:", round((na2 - na1) /
sum(!is.na(var_name))*100, 1), "n")
+
      cat("Mean of the outliers:", round(mo, 2), "n")
+
      m2 <- mean(var_name, na.rm = T)
+
      cat("Mean without removing outliers:", round(m1, 2), "n")
+
      cat("Mean if we remove outliers:", round(m2, 2), "n")
+
      response <- readline(prompt="Do you want to remove outliers and
to replace with NA? [yes/no]: ")
+
      if(response == "y" | response == "yes"){
+
      dt[as.character(substitute(var))] <- invisible(var_name)
+
      assign(as.character(as.list(match.call())$dt), dt, envir =
.GlobalEnv)
+
      cat("Outliers successfully removed", "n")
+
       return(invisible(dt))
+
      } else{
+
      cat("Nothing changed", "n")
+
      return(invisible(var_name))
+
      }}
> outlierKD(Autompg,displacement)
 Outliers identified: 0 nPropotion (%) of outliers: 0 nMean of the
outliers: NaN nMean without
 removing outliers: 193.43 nMean if we remove outliers: 193.43 n
 Do you want to remove outliers and to replace with NA? [yes/no]:
 yes
 Outliers successfully removed
```

For now, if we want to check the outliers for RH and AH, the preceding command is executed and the outputs generated are given as follows:

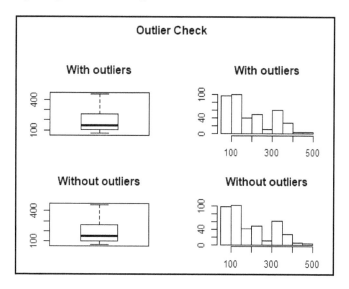

Grubbs test is basically a test undertaken with statistics to identify the outliers in a univariate dataset, and even multi-factor datasets that are assumed to have come from a normally distributed population. The following steps are used to evaluate the data frame with core attributes of AH and RH:

1. Install the outliers package as follows, which helps in detecting outliers for the column specified:

```
> install.packages("outliers")
Installing package into 'C:/Users/Radhika/Documents/R/win-
library/3.5'
(as 'lib' is unspecified)
trying URL
'https://cran.rstudio.com/bin/windows/contrib/3.5/outliers_0.14.zip
'
Content type 'application/zip' length 83897 bytes (81 KB)
downloaded 81 KB
package 'outliers' successfully unpacked and MD5 sums checked
he downloaded binary packages are in
C:\Users\Radhika\AppData\Local\Temp\Rtmpc1oW5p\downloaded_packages
```

2. Include the necessary libraries to calculate the Grubbs test as follows:

```
> library(outliers)
 Warning message:
package 'outliers' was built under R version 3.5.2
>
            library(ggplot2)
```

3. Create a function for generating flag values of outliers. This function follows the Grubbs test condition:

```
> grubbs.flag <- function(x) {
+
            outliers <- NULL
+
            test <- x
+
            grubbs.result <- grubbs.test(test)
+
            pv <- grubbs.result$p.value
 +
            while(pv < 0.05) {
 +
                outliers <-
c(outliers,as.numeric(strsplit(grubbs.result$alternative,"
")[[1]][3]))
    +
                test <- x[!x %in% outliers]
    +
                grubbs.result <- grubbs.test(test)
    +
                pv <- grubbs.result$p.value
    +
            }
    +
            return(data.frame(X=x,Outlier=(x %in% outliers)))
    +
}
```

4. Call the respective function to analyze the value interpretation of AH and RH, as shown here:

```
> grubbs.flag(AirQualityUCI$AH)
> grubbs.flag(Autompg$displacement)
                X Outlier
1 307.0 FALSE
2 350.0 FALSE
3 318.0 FALSE
```

```
4  304.0  FALSE
5  302.0  FALSE
6  429.0  FALSE
7  454.0  FALSE
8  440.0  FALSE
9  455.0  FALSE
10  390.0  FALSE
11  383.0  FALSE
12  340.0  FALSE
13  400.0  FALSE
14  455.0  FALSE
15  113.0  FALSE
16  198.0  FALSE
```

And if you want a histogram with different colors, you can use the following command:

```
> >
ggplot(grubbs.flag(Autompg$displacement),aes(x=Autompg$displacement
,color=Outlier,fill=Outlier))+
+
geom_histogram(binwidth=diff(range(Autompg$displacement))/30)+
theme_bw()
        >
```

This gives us the following output plot:

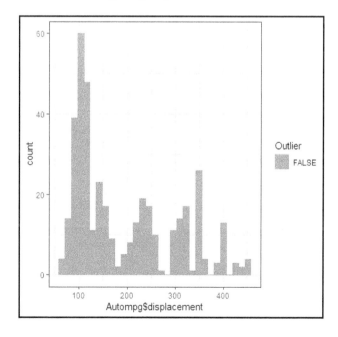

Parsimonious model

Parsimonious models are simple models with great explanatory predictive power. They usually explain data with a minimum number of parameters, or predictor variables. `MoEClust` is the required R package that fits finite Gaussian Mixtures of Experts models using a range of parsimonious covariance with the help of EM/CEM algorithms.

The following steps are implemented to create a parsimonious model with a visual representation:

1. Install the following package, which is needed to create a parsimonious model of our automobile `Autompg` dataset:

```
> install.packages('devtools')
Installing package into 'C:/Users/Radhika/Documents/R/win-
library/3.5'
        (as 'lib' is unspecified)
        trying URL
'https://cran.rstudio.com/bin/windows/contrib/3.5/devtools_2.0.2.zi
p'
        Content type 'application/zip' length 383720 bytes (374
KB)
        downloaded 374 KB
        package 'devtools' successfully unpacked and MD5 sums
checked
        The downloaded binary packages are in
C:\Users\Radhika\AppData\Local\Temp\Rtmpc1oW5p\downloaded_packages
        >
        install.packages('MoEClust')
        Installing package into
'C:/Users/Radhika/Documents/R/win-library/3.5'
        (as 'lib' is unspecified)
        trying URL
'https://cran.rstudio.com/bin/windows/contrib/3.5/MoEClust_1.2.1.zi
p'
        Content type 'application/zip' length 759555 bytes (741
KB)
        downloaded 741 KB
        package 'MoEClust' successfully unpacked and MD5 sums
checked
        The downloaded binary packages are in
C:\Users\Radhika\AppData\Local\Temp\Rtmpc1oW5p\downloaded_packages
        >
        library(MoEClust)
```

```
   __  __   ____   ____    _  _
  | \/ | |  ___/ _ \ | | | Gaussian Parsimonious
  | .. | |__  | |_  | / \/ |_ _ ___| |_ Clustering Models
  | |\/| |/ _ \| __|| | | | | | / _| _| with Covariates
  | | | | (_) | |___| \_/\ | |_| \_ \ |_
  \_| |_/\___/\____/ \____/_|\__,_|___/\__| version 1.2.1
          Type '?MoEClust' to see a brief guide to how to use this
  R package.
          Type 'citation("MoEClust")' for citing the package in
  publications.
          Type 'MoE_news()' to see new features recent changes and
  bug fixes.
          Warning message:
          package 'MoEClust' was built under R version 3.5.3
```

This package helps in clustering the data as per the required value analysis.

2. Variables created include attributes for calculating the rate of acceleration with respect to displacement as follows:

```
> View(Autompg)
> mpg <- Autompg[,1]
> displacement <- Autompg[,3]
> Acceleration <- Autompg[,6]
> dim(Autompg)
[1] 398 9
```

3. For models that covariate in the gating network, or models with equal mixing proportions, there is no need to fit single component models:

```
> m1     <- MoE_clust(displacement, G=0:2, verbose=FALSE)
> m1
          Call: MoE_clust(data = displacement, G = 0:2, verbose =
  FALSE)
          Best Model (according to BIC): univariate, unequal
  variance (V), with 2 components
          BIC = -4584.632 | ICL = -4622.174 | AIC = -4564.7
          No covariates
> m2 <- MoE_clust(displacement, G=2:16, verbose=FALSE)
> m2
          Call: MoE_clust(data = displacement, G = 2:16, verbose =
  FALSE)
          Best Model (according to BIC): univariate, unequal
  variance (V), with 12 components
          BIC = -4264.453 | ICL = -4293.686 | AIC = -4124.927
          No covariates

> comp <- MoE_compare(m1, m2)
```

4. This step involves a comparison of the data values and the covariates required, as shown here:

```
> comp <- MoE_compare(m1, m2)
> comp
----------------------------------------------------------------
-----------
Comparison of Gaussian Parsimonious Clustering Models with
Covariates
Data: displacement
----------------------------------------------------------------
-----------
rank MoENames modelNames G df iters bic icl aic loglik gating
expert
1 m2 V 12 35 103 -4264.453 -4293.686 -4124.927 -2027.463 None None
2 m2 V 15 44 107 -4283.584 -4291.018 -4108.18 -2010.09 None None
3 m2 V 11 32 86 -4305.753 -4335.053 -4178.186 -2057.093 None None
equalPro
FALSE
FALSE
FALSE
```

5. Convert the `MoEClust` class to the `Mclust` class in order to visualize the results with respect to the two options that are required, as shown in the following code:

```
> (mod <- as.Mclust(comp$optimal))
'Mclust' model object: (V,12)
        Available components:
        [1] "call" "data" "modelName" "n" "d"
        [6] "G" "BIC" "bic" "loglik" "df"
        [11] "hypvol" "parameters" "z" "classification"
"uncertainty"
> plot(mod, what="classification")
> plot(mod, what="uncertainty")
```

The following plot that has been created refers to the clustering pattern of `classification`:

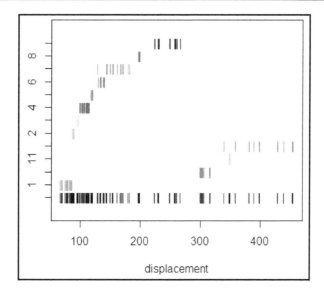

The plot shown here refers to the clustering pattern of `uncertainty`:

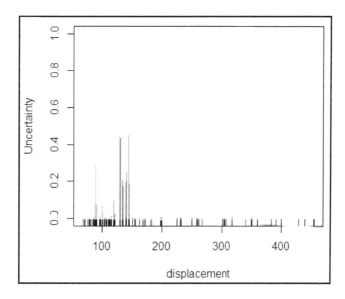

Multi-factor variance analysis

To understand the correlation between the variables, it is important to understand the interaction between all the variables within the dataset. Let's focus on multi-factor variance analysis of the data frame specified with the help of the following steps:

1. Create an aggregate value of the data frame with respect to the `mpg` and `displacement` values mentioned as follows:

```
> d <- aggregate(mpg ~ displacement, data = Autompg, FUN = mean)

> d
            displacement mpg
1  68.0  29.00000
2  70.0  20.23333
3  71.0  31.50000
4  72.0  35.00000
5  76.0  31.00000
6  78.0  32.80000
7  79.0  32.18333
8  80.0  21.50000
9  81.0  35.10000
10 83.0  32.00000
>
print(abs(d[[2]][1]-d[[2]][2]))
[1] 8.7666
```
   67

2. Now, let's build a model with the `lm` function to examine the coefficient for regression analysis. These coefficients include attributes required in the dataset, as shown in the following code:

```
> fit0 <- lm(mpg ~ displacement, data = Autompg)
> fit0
            Call:
            lm(formula = mpg ~ displacement, data = Autompg)
            Coefficients:
             (Intercept) displacement
                 35.17475 -0.06028
> lm(formula = mpg ~ displacement, data = Autompg)
            Call:
            lm(formula = mpg ~ displacement, data = Autompg)
            Coefficients:
             (Intercept) displacement
                 35.17475 -0.06028
```

In the preceding model, we try to gauge the meaning of coefficients. The intercept stands for the mean of the displacement variant, and if we add the intercept to the coefficient indicated, then we get the average of the manual variants.

3. Now, it is important to build the respective models as per the required standards. The following model creation will help us to focus on multi-factor variance analysis:

```
> fit0 <- lm(mpg ~ displacement, data = Autompg)
> fit1 <- lm(mpg ~ ., data = Autompg)

> fit2 <- lm(mpg ~ Acceleration + weight, Autompg)

> View(Autompg)

> fit3 <- lm(mpg ~ displacement + horsepower + Acceleration +
weight, Autompg)

> fit0

Call:

lm(formula = mpg ~ displacement, data = Autompg)

Coefficients:

(Intercept) displacement

35.17475 -0.06028

> fit1

Call:

lm(formula = mpg ~ ., data = Autompg)

Coefficients:

(Intercept) cylinders4

-9.352043 7.081991

cylinders5 cylinders6

10.098408 4.129151

cylinders8 displacement
```

```
3.482500 0.003262

horsepower weight

-0.045326 -0.004168

acceleration model.year

-0.469028 0.622968

origin CarNameamc ambassador dpl

1.236845 3.399253

CarNameamc ambassador sst CarNameamc concord

3.285919 0.295866

CarNameamc concord d/l CarNameamc concord dl 6

-0.611860 0.439782

CarNameamc gremlin CarNameamc hornet

0.531260 1.214846

CarNameamc hornet sportabout (sw) CarNameamc matador

0.577841 0.983407

CarNameamc matador (sw) CarNameamc pacer

3.013232

> fit2

Call:

lm(formula = mpg ~ Acceleration + weight, data = Autompg)

Coefficients:

(Intercept) Acceleration weight

41.399828 0.250816 -0.007336

> fit3
```

```
Call:

lm(formula = mpg ~ displacement + horsepower + Acceleration +

weight, data = Autompg)

Coefficients:

(Intercept) displacement horsepower Acceleration weight

45.251140 -0.006001 -0.043608 -0.023148 -0.005281

> anova(fit0, fit1, fit2, fit3)
```

4. Understanding the uncertainty of the best model to show the results as needed is important:

```
> confint(fit3)
2.5 % 97.5 %
        (Intercept) 40.422278855 50.080000544
        displacement -0.019192122 0.007190380
        horsepower -0.076193029 -0.011022433
        Acceleration -0.270094049 0.223798050
        weight -0.006874738 -0.003686277
```

5. Creating visualized models of the data plots that are being created is also equally important. It is important to focus on **Aikaike Information Criterium** (**AIC**) scores.

A lower AIC implies a better model.

6. We can analyze the AIC values calculated using the following print function for each model:

```
> print(AIC(fit0))
 [1] 2357.044
> print(AIC(fit1))
[1] 1768.663
> print(AIC(fit2))
[1] 2296.307
> print(AIC(fit3))
[1] 2253.195
```

7. A box plot can be used to analyze the number of cars with the same origin. As you can see with the origin column, there are three values included, namely, one, two, and three, to detect the origin of the automobiles that are being tracked. We can use the box plot mentioned as follows to track the origin type of automobiles with specific names of `First`, `Second`, and `Third`:

```
> boxplot(mpg ~ origin, data = Autompg, names = c("First",
"Second", "Third"))
```

This gives us the following output plot:

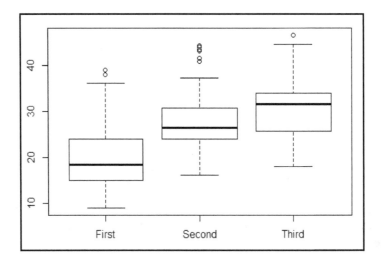

Exploring graphically the dataset

In this section, we will focus on exploring the dataset graphically using a DOE scatter plot, a DOE mean plot, a DOE standard deviation plot, and a contour plot. Let's focus on each of them in turn:

1. In this step, we will depict the scatter plot in two ways. A scatter plot shows the relationship between `wt` and `mpg` as follows:

```
> plot(Autompg$weight , Autompg$mpg, xlab = 'Weight of Cars', ylab
= 'Miles per Gallon', main = 'Scatter Plot for MTCars Weight Vs
MPG')
```

This gives us the following output plot:

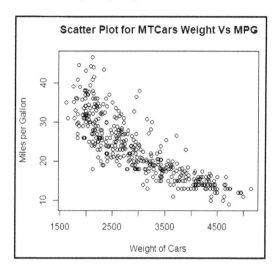

The alternative way to depict the scatter plot is with the help of the `ggplot2` package or library, which is achieved by executing the following command:

```
> library(ggplot2)
> ggplot(data=Autompg,aes(x=weight, y=mpg)) + geom_point() +
theme_minimal()
```

This gives us the following output plot:

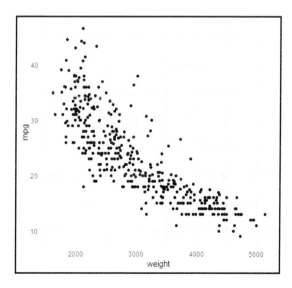

2. This step involves the creation of the mean plot. The `gplots` package includes all of the functions required to create a mean plot, shown as follows:

```
> library(gplots)

Attaching package: 'gplots'
        The following object is masked from 'package:stats':
            lowess
        Warning message:
        package 'gplots' was built under R version 3.5.2
> plotmeans(model.year ~ origin, data = Autompg, frame = FALSE)
There were 17 warnings (use warnings() to see them)
```

Consider that we have to plot the data with the model of the car and the year of origin. We can achieve this as shown in the following screenshot, which is considered a suitable mean plot:

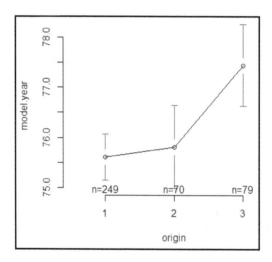

3. Here, we will focus on the standard deviation plot, which is important from an error generation point of view. The standard deviation of an observation variable is the square root of its variance, as shown in the following code:

```
> rate_of_activity = Autompg$displacement
 There were 12 warnings (use warnings() to see them)
> sd(rate_of_activity)
[1] 104.2698
```

The variations in the standard deviation plot are depicted as follows:

```
>  ggplot(Autompg, aes(x=mpg, y=displacement)) +
 +
             geom_bar(stat="identity", color="black",
position=position_dodge())
```

This gives us the following output plot:

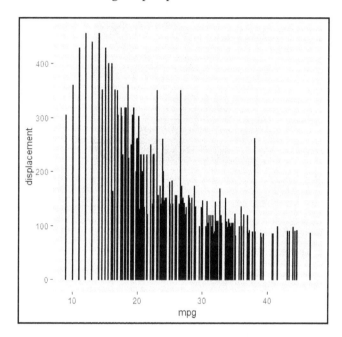

4. This involves creating 2D contour plots to establish the relationship between three or more variables, as shown in the following code:

```
> p <- ggplot(Autompg, aes(x = weight, y = displacement))
> p + geom_point() | stat_density2d()
> p + stat_density2d(aes(colour = ..level..))
> p + stat_density2d(aes(fill = ..density..), geom = "raster",
contour = FALSE)
```

This gives us the following density plot:

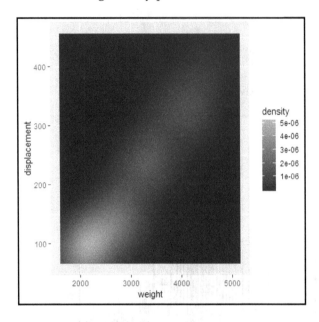

The following plot is created if we request activation for contours to be represented in the given density plot:

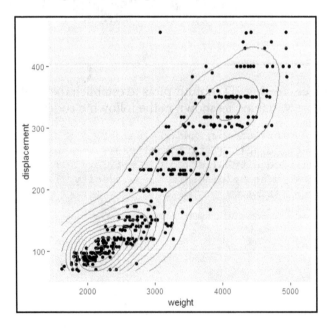

Once the contours are set as `False` or deactivated, we get the following plot:

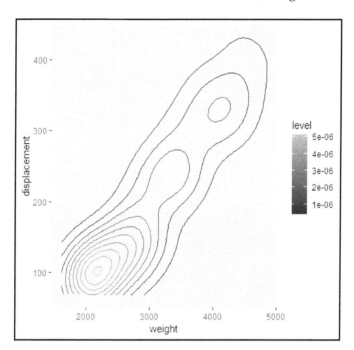

Summary

In this chapter, we have focused on the implementation of all libraries of a multi-factor dataset, which is strongly linked to various data type values. The best demonstration is to check various parameters of automobiles, especially with reference to mpg, displacement, and acceleration, including weight parameters. We have listed some of the various packages that are available for reading, in various kinds of attributes, within the dataset specified in R. There are lots of different options, and even the options we have listed have a wide functionality that we are going to cover and use as we go further into this book.

In the next chapter, we will introduce a dataset from the regression problem category and explain how to use exploratory data analysis techniques to analyze this data.

10
Handling Optimization and Regression Data Problems

This chapter will introduce a dataset from the regression problem category and teach us how to use exploratory data analysis techniques to analyze this data. We will learn and use the exploratory data analysis techniques of the scatter plot, 6-plot, linear correlation plot, linear intercept plot, linear slope plot, and linear residual standard deviation plot. We will also explore and analyze a real world dataset called the Glass Identification dataset from UCI.

The following topics will be covered in this chapter:

- Introducing and reading data
- Cleaning and tidying up data
- Mapping and understanding the underlying structure of the dataset and identifying the most important variables
- Testing assumptions and hypothesis, estimating parameters, and calculating the margins of error
- Creating a list of outliers or other anomalies
- Uncovering a parsimonious model
- Exploring the dataset graphically using a scatter plot, 6-plot, linear correlation plot, linear intercept plot, linear slope plot, and linear residual standard deviation plot

Technical requirements

You should have hands-on experience or knowledge of the following points before getting started with this chapter:

- R programming language
- RStudio
- R packages
  (including `readr`, `readxl`, `jsonlite`, `httr`, `rvest`, `DBI`, `dplyr`, `stringr`, `forcats`, `lubridate`, `hms`, `blob`, `ggplot2`, and `knitr`)

Introducing and reading a dataset

The Glass Identification dataset from UCI contains 10 attributes, including the ID, which is regarded as a primary key. The response is a glass type, which has seven discrete values. The following is taken from the website:

The study of classification of types of glass was motivated by criminological investigation. At the scene of the crime, the glass left can be used as evidence.

You can download the dataset from the following
link: `https://github.com/PacktPublishing/Hands-On-Exploratory-Data-Analysis-with-R/tree/master/ch10`.

The user can refer to the following link for more information regarding the dataset: `https://archive.ics.uci.edu/ml/datasets/glass+identification`.

This section is all about understanding the dataset and its attributes. We will implement the following steps, as we did in the previous chapters, to understand the attribute structure, or rather, metadata information pertaining to the dataset:

1. The first step involves importing the dataset from the URL in the R workspace indicated, as shown in the following code:

```
> library(readr)
> library(readxl)
> GlassDataset <- read_xlsx("Glass.xlsx")
> GlassDataset

# A tibble: 214 x 11
Id RI Na Mg Al Si K Ca Ba Fe Type
<dbl>
```

```
<dbl>
<dbl>
<dbl>
<dbl>
<dbl>
<dbl>
<dbl>
<dbl>
<dbl>
<dbl>

 1  1 1.52 13.6 4.49 1.1  71.8 0.06 8.75 0 0    1
 2  2 1.52 13.9 3.6  1.36 72.7 0.48 7.83 0 0    1
 3  3 1.52 13.5 3.55 1.54 73.0 0.39 7.78 0 0    1
 4  4 1.52 13.2 3.69 1.29 72.6 0.570 8.22 0 0   1
 5  5 1.52 13.3 3.62 1.24 73.1 0.55 8.07 0 0    1
 6  6 1.52 12.8 3.61 1.62 73.0 0.64 8.07 0 0.26 1
 7  7 1.52 13.3 3.6  1.14 73.1 0.580 8.17 0 0   1
 8  8 1.52 13.2 3.61 1.05 73.2 0.570 8.24 0 0   1
 9  9 1.52 14.0 3.58 1.37 72.1 0.56 8.3  0 0    1
 10 10 1.52 13 3.6   1.36 73.0 0.570 8.4 0 0.11 1

 # ... with 204 more rows
 > View(GlassDataset)
```

The dataset is shown as follows:

Id	RI	Na	Mg	Al	Si	K	Ca	Ba	Fe	Type
1	1	1.52101	13.64	4.49	1.10	71.78	0.06	8.75	0.00	0.00	1
2	2	1.51761	13.89	3.60	1.36	72.73	0.48	7.83	0.00	0.00	1
3	3	1.51618	13.53	3.55	1.54	72.99	0.39	7.78	0.00	0.00	1
4	4	1.51766	13.21	3.69	1.29	72.61	0.57	8.22	0.00	0.00	1
5	5	1.51742	13.27	3.62	1.24	73.08	0.55	8.07	0.00	0.00	1
6	6	1.51596	12.79	3.61	1.62	72.97	0.64	8.07	0.00	0.26	1
7	7	1.51743	13.30	3.60	1.14	73.09	0.58	8.17	0.00	0.00	1
8	8	1.51756	13.15	3.61	1.05	73.24	0.57	8.24	0.00	0.00	1
9	9	1.51918	14.04	3.58	1.37	72.08	0.56	8.30	0.00	0.00	1
10	10	1.51755	13.00	3.60	1.36	72.99	0.57	8.40	0.00	0.11	1
11	11	1.51571	12.72	3.46	1.56	73.20	0.67	8.09	0.00	0.24	1

GlassDataset ×

Filter

Showing 1 to 11 of 214 entries

2. Now, focus on the structure of the data frame with the required function, namely, str():

```
> str(GlassDataset)
> str(GlassDataset)

Classes 'tbl_df', 'tbl' and 'data.frame': 214 obs. of 11 variables:
$ Id  : num 1 2 3 4 5 6 7 8 9 10 ...
$ RI  : num 1.52 1.52 1.52 1.52 1.52 ...
$ Na  : num 13.6 13.9 13.5 13.2 13.3 ...
$ Mg  : num 4.49 3.6 3.55 3.69 3.62 3.61 3.6 3.61 3.58 3.6 ...
$ Al  : num 1.1 1.36 1.54 1.29 1.24 1.62 1.14 1.05 1.37 1.36 ...
$ Si  : num 71.8 72.7 73 72.6 73.1 ...
$ K   : num 0.06 0.48 0.39 0.57 0.55 0.64 0.58 0.57 0.56 0.57 ...
$ Ca  : num 8.75 7.83 7.78 8.22 8.07 8.07 8.17 8.24 8.3 8.4 ...
$ Ba  : num 0 0 0 0 0 0 0 0 0 0 ...
$ Fe  : num 0 0 0 0 0 0.26 0 0 0 0.11 ...
$ Type: num 1 1 1 1 1 1 1 1 1 1 ...
```

Now let's discuss the attribute names and their description of our dataset, or rather our data frame, as shown in the following table:

Attribute	Description
Id	A unique identification number from 1 to 214
RI	Refers to the refractive index
Na	Refers to the sodium measurement
Mg	Refers to the magnesium measurement
AI	Refers to the aluminium measurement
Si	Refers to the silicon measurement
K	Refers to the potassium measurement
Ca	Refers to the calcium measurement
Ba	Refers to the barium measurement
Fe	Refers to the iron measurement

Type	This is a class attribute where each numerical value includes some of the following representation: • 1: `building_windows_float_processed` • 2: `building_windows_non_float_processed` • 3: `vehicle_windows_float_processed` • 4: `vehicle_windows_non_float_processed` (none in this database) • 5: `Containers` • 6: `Tableware` • 7: `Headlamps`

Cleaning the dataset

Data cleaning, or rather, tidying up the data is the process of transforming raw data into specific consistent data, which includes analysis in a simpler manner. The R programming language includes a set of comprehensive tools that are specifically designed to clean the data in an effective manner. We will focus on cleaning the dataset over here in a specific way.

The following steps are carried out to perform cleaning attributes of datasets or data frames:

1. Include the libraries that are required to clean and tidy up the dataset as follows:

```
> library(dplyr)
> library(tidyr)
```

2. Analyze the `summary` of our dataset as shown here, which will help us to focus on which attributes we need to work on:

```
> summary(GlassDataset)
Id RI Na Mg Al Si

Min. : 1.00 Min. :1.511 Min. :10.73 Min. :0.000 Min. :0.290 Min.
:69.81

1st Qu.: 54.25 1st Qu.:1.517 1st Qu.:12.91 1st Qu.:2.115 1st
Qu.:1.190 1st Qu.:72.28

Median :107.50 Median :1.518 Median :13.30 Median :3.480 Median
:1.360 Median :72.79

Mean :107.50 Mean :1.518 Mean :13.41 Mean :2.685 Mean :1.445 Mean
:72.65
```

3rd Qu.:160.75 3rd Qu.:1.519 3rd Qu.:13.82 3rd Qu.:3.600 3rd Qu.:1.630 3rd Qu.:73.09

Max. :214.00 Max. :1.534 Max. :17.38 Max. :4.490 Max. :3.500 Max. :75.41

K Ca Ba Fe Type

Min. :0.0000 Min. : 5.430 Min. :0.000 Min. :0.00000 Min. :1.00

1st Qu.:0.1225 1st Qu.: 8.240 1st Qu.:0.000 1st Qu.:0.00000 1st Qu.:1.00

Median :0.5550 Median : 8.600 Median :0.000 Median :0.00000 Median :2.00

Mean :0.4971 Mean : 8.957 Mean :0.175 Mean :0.05701 Mean :2.78

3rd Qu.:0.6100 3rd Qu.: 9.172 3rd Qu.:0.000 3rd Qu.:0.10000 3rd Qu.:3.00

Max. :6.2100 Max. :16.190 Max. :3.150 Max. :0.51000 Max. :7.00

3. Let's view the first 6 columns and last 6 columns of data by executing the following command:

```
> head(GlassDataset)
# A tibble: 6 x 11
```

Id RI Na Mg Al Si K Ca Ba Fe Type

```
<dbl>
<dbl>
<dbl>
<dbl>
<dbl>
<dbl>
<dbl>
<dbl>
<dbl>
<dbl>
<dbl>
```

```
1 1 1.52 13.6 4.49 1.1 71.8 0.06 8.75 0 0 1
2 2 1.52 13.9 3.6 1.36 72.7 0.48 7.83 0 0 1
3 3 1.52 13.5 3.55 1.54 73.0 0.39 7.78 0 0 1
4 4 1.52 13.2 3.69 1.29 72.6 0.570 8.22 0 0 1
5 5 1.52 13.3 3.62 1.24 73.1 0.55 8.07 0 0 1
```

```
6 6 1.52 12.8 3.61 1.62 73.0 0.64 8.07 0 0.26 1

> tail(GlassDataset)

# A tibble: 6 x 11
Id RI Na Mg Al Si K Ca Ba Fe Type

<dbl>
<dbl>
<dbl>
<dbl>
<dbl>
<dbl>
<dbl>
<dbl>
<dbl>
<dbl>
<dbl>

1 209 1.52 14.4 0 2.74 72.8 0 9.45 0.54 0 7
2 210 1.52 14.1 0 2.88 72.6 0.08 9.18 1.06 0 7
3 211 1.52 14.9 0 1.99 73.1 0 8.4 1.59 0 7
4 212 1.52 14.4 0 2.02 73.4 0 8.44 1.64 0 7
5 213 1.52 14.4 0 1.94 73.6 0 8.48 1.57 0 7
6 214 1.52 14.2 0 2.08 73.4 0 8.62 1.67 0 7
```

4. Based on the results of the preceding `str(cars)` function, it is observed that several issues with how the `read.csv` function imported the data need to be clarified before proceeding in-depth with the analysis.:

```
> str(GlassDataset)
Classes 'tbl_df', 'tbl' and 'data.frame': 214 obs. of 11 variables:

$ Id : num 1 2 3 4 5 6 7 8 9 10 ...
$ RI : num 1.52 1.52 1.52 1.52 1.52 ...
$ Na : num 13.6 13.9 13.5 13.2 13.3 ...
$ Mg : num 4.49 3.6 3.55 3.69 3.62 3.61 3.6 3.61 3.58 3.6 ...
$ Al : num 1.1 1.36 1.54 1.29 1.24 1.62 1.14 1.05 1.37 1.36 ...
$ Si : num 71.8 72.7 73 72.6 73.1 ...
$ K : num 0.06 0.48 0.39 0.57 0.55 0.64 0.58 0.57 0.56 0.57 ...
$ Ca : num 8.75 7.83 7.78 8.22 8.07 8.07 8.17 8.24 8.3 8.4 ...
$ Ba : num 0 0 0 0 0 0 0 0 0 0 ...
$ Fe : num 0 0 0 0 0 0.26 0 0 0 0.11 ...
$ Type: num 1 1 1 1 1 1 1 1 1 1 ...

> GlassDataset$Type = GlassDataset$Type %>% factor(labels =
sort(unique(GlassDataset$Type)))
> View(GlassDataset)
```

This gives us the following output:

GlassDataset

Filter

	Id	RI	Na	Mg	Al	Si	K	Ca	Ba	Fe	Type
1	1	1.52101	13.64	4.49	1.10	71.78	0.06	8.75	0.00	0.00	1
2	2	1.51761	13.89	3.60	1.36	72.73	0.48	7.83	0.00	0.00	1
3	3	1.51618	13.53	3.55	1.54	72.99	0.39	7.78	0.00	0.00	1
4	4	1.51766	13.21	3.69	1.29	72.61	0.57	8.22	0.00	0.00	1
5	5	1.51742	13.27	3.62	1.24	73.08	0.55	8.07	0.00	0.00	1
6	6	1.51596	12.79	3.61	1.62	72.97	0.64	8.07	0.00	0.26	1
7	7	1.51743	13.30	3.60	1.14	73.09	0.58	8.17	0.00	0.00	1
8	8	1.51756	13.15	3.61	1.05	73.24	0.57	8.24	0.00	0.00	1
9	9	1.51918	14.04	3.58	1.37	72.08	0.56	8.30	0.00	0.00	1
10	10	1.51755	13.00	3.60	1.36	72.99	0.57	8.40	0.00	0.11	1
11	11	1.51571	12.72	3.46	1.56	73.20	0.67	8.09	0.00	0.24	1

Showing 1 to 11 of 214 entries

Mapping and understanding the data structure

This section involves understanding the depth of each and every attribute that is considered to be important for the dataset indicated:

1. To get a feel for the data as per the attribute structure, use the following code:

```
> class(GlassDataset)
[1] "tbl_df" "tbl" "data.frame"
```

The output shows that the dataset is merely a tabular format of the data frame.

2. Check the dimensions of the dataset as follows:

```
> dim(GlassDataset)
[1] 214 11
```

This means that the dataset comprises 214 rows and 11 columns. The column structure is as discussed in the first section.

3. View the column names of the dataset and check whether they correspond to the records included in the Excel file:

```
> colnames(GlassDataset)
[1] "Id" "RI" "Na" "Mg" "Al" "Si" "K" "Ca" "Ba" "Fe" "Type"
```

4. Check the structure of the GlassDataset dataset by executing the following commands:

```
> str(GlassDataset)
Classes 'tbl_df', 'tbl' and 'data.frame': 214 obs. of 11 variables:

$ Id : num 1 2 3 4 5 6 7 8 9 10 ...
$ RI : num 1.52 1.52 1.52 1.52 1.52 ...
$ Na : num 13.6 13.9 13.5 13.2 13.3 ...
$ Mg : num 4.49 3.6 3.55 3.69 3.62 3.61 3.6 3.61 3.58 3.6 ...
$ Al : num 1.1 1.36 1.54 1.29 1.24 1.62 1.14 1.05 1.37 1.36 ...
$ Si : num 71.8 72.7 73 72.6 73.1 ...
$ K : num 0.06 0.48 0.39 0.57 0.55 0.64 0.58 0.57 0.56 0.57 ...
$ Ca : num 8.75 7.83 7.78 8.22 8.07 8.07 8.17 8.24 8.3 8.4 ...
$ Ba : num 0 0 0 0 0 0 0 0 0 0 ...
$ Fe : num 0 0 0 0 0 0.26 0 0 0 0.11 ...
$ Type: Factor w/ 6 levels "1","2","3","5",..: 1 1 1 1 1 1 1 1 1 1
...
```

The structure depicts a data type for each column and the values associated with it, such as numerical or decimal format.

5. We will now check the structure using the dplyr package as follows:

```
> library(dplyr)
> library(dplyr)

> glimpse(GlassDataset)

Observations: 214

Variables: 11

$ Id <dbl> 1, 2, 3, 4, 5, 6, 7, 8, 9, 10, 11, 12, 13, 14, 15, 16,
17, 18, 19, 20, 21, 22, 23,...

$ RI <dbl> 1.52101, 1.51761, 1.51618, 1.51766, 1.51742, 1.51596,
1.51743, 1.51756, 1.51918, 1...
```

```
$ Na <dbl> 13.64, 13.89, 13.53, 13.21, 13.27, 12.79, 13.30, 13.15,
14.04, 13.00, 12.72, 12.80...

$ Mg <dbl> 4.49, 3.60, 3.55, 3.69, 3.62, 3.61, 3.60, 3.61, 3.58,
3.60, 3.46, 3.66, 3.43, 3.56...

$ Al <dbl> 1.10, 1.36, 1.54, 1.29, 1.24, 1.62, 1.14, 1.05, 1.37,
1.36, 1.56, 1.27, 1.40, 1.27...

$ Si <dbl> 71.78, 72.73, 72.99, 72.61, 73.08, 72.97, 73.09, 73.24,
72.08, 72.99, 73.20, 73.01...

$ K <dbl> 0.06, 0.48, 0.39, 0.57, 0.55, 0.64, 0.58, 0.57, 0.56,
0.57, 0.67, 0.60, 0.69, 0.54...

$ Ca <dbl> 8.75, 7.83, 7.78, 8.22, 8.07, 8.07, 8.17, 8.24, 8.30,
8.40, 8.09, 8.56, 8.05, 8.38...

$ Ba <dbl> 0.00, 0.00, 0.00, 0.00, 0.00, 0.00, 0.00, 0.00, 0.00,
0.00, 0.00, 0.00, 0.00, 0.00...

$ Fe <dbl> 0.00, 0.00, 0.00, 0.00, 0.00, 0.26, 0.00, 0.00, 0.00,
0.11, 0.24, 0.00, 0.24, 0.17...

$ Type <fct> 1, 1, 1, 1, 1, 1, 1, 1, 1, 1, 1, 1, 1, 1, 1, 1, 1, 1,
1, 1, 1, 1, 1, 1, 1, 1, 1, 1...
```

The `glimpse()` function makes it possible to have a look at each and every column of the data frame. This is similar to the `str()` function, the only difference being that it displays more data than the `str()` function, which is normally used to obtain the structure of the data.

6. Plot the important parameters of our data frame, which focuses on calculating the rate of speed using acceleration and displacement parameters, demonstrated as follows:

```
> plot(GlassDataset$Id, GlassDataset$Type, main = "Type of Glass",
xlab = "Identification Number", ylab = "Type")
```

This gives us the following output plot:

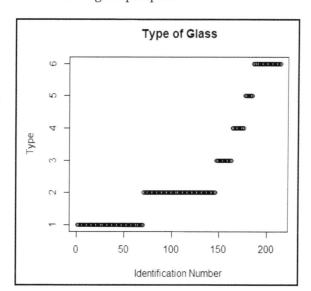

Hypothesis test

This section is all about hypothesis testing in R. This testing is merely an assumption made by the researcher about the population of data collected in relation to any experiment. As a first step, we will introduce the statistical hypothesis in R, and later, we will cover the decision error in R with a single t-test and directional hypothesis in R.

t-test in R

This is also referred to as the student's t-test, which is a method for comparing two samples. It can usually be implemented to determine whether the samples are proper or different. This is considered a parametric test, and the data should be distributed normally.

R can handle the various versions of the t-test using the t.test() command.

The following command is used for our GlassDataset dataset to check the parameters of patients with a specific age range who have undergone a biopsy test:

```
> t.test(GlassDataset$RI, GlassDataset$Type)

Welch Two Sample t-test
```

```
data: GlassDataset$RI and GlassDataset$Type

t = -8.7756, df = 213, p-value = 5.559e-16

alternative hypothesis: true difference in means is not equal to 0

95 percent confidence interval:

-1.5454790 -0.9785378

sample estimates:

mean of x mean of y

1.518365 2.780374
```

The t.test() command is generally used to compare two vectors of numerical values. The vectors can be specified in a variety of ways, depending on how your data objects are set out.

Directional hypothesis in R

In this hypothesis testing, you can only specify a direction to the dataset mentioned previously. Here, we will use the same function with the alternative equal to (=) instruction to switch the emphasis from a two-sided test (the default) to a one-sided test. The choices that we have are two.sided, less, or greater, and the choice can be abbreviated, as shown in the following command:

```
> t.test(GlassDataset$RI, mu = 5, alternative = 'greater')
One Sample t-test

data: GlassDataset$RI

t = -16771, df = 213, p-value = 1

alternative hypothesis: true mean is greater than 5

95 percent confidence interval:

1.518022 Inf

sample estimates:

mean of x
```

```
1.518365

> t.test(GlassDataset$Type, mu = 5, alternative = 'greater')

One Sample t-test

data: GlassDataset$Type

t = -15.435, df = 213, p-value = 1

alternative hypothesis: true mean is greater than 5

95 percent confidence interval:

2.542796 Inf

sample estimates:

mean of x

2.780374
```

It is clear that the values generated include sample estimates and the mean of x and is calculated as 02.780374 for understanding the type of glass type required. This also means that the error generated is quite low in comparison to other attributes.

Grubbs' test and checking outliers

In statistics, or particularly in R programming, an **outlier** is defined as an observation that is far removed from most of the other observations. Often an outlier is present due to a measurement error.

The following script is used to detect the particular outliers for each and every attribute:

```
> outlierKD <- function(dt, var) {
 +
         var_name <- eval(substitute(var),eval(dt))
         +
         na1 <- sum(is.na(var_name))
         +
         m1 <- mean(var_name, na.rm = T)
         +
         par(mfrow=c(2, 2), oma=c(0,0,3,0))
         +
         boxplot(var_name, main="With outliers")
```

```
+
hist(var_name, main="With outliers", xlab=NA, ylab=NA)
+
outlier <- boxplot.stats(var_name)$out
+
mo <- mean(outlier)
+
var_name <- ifelse(var_name %in% outlier, NA, var_name)
+
boxplot(var_name, main="Without outliers")
+
hist(var_name, main="Without outliers", xlab=NA, ylab=NA)
+
title("Outlier Check", outer=TRUE)
+
na2 <- sum(is.na(var_name))
+
cat("Outliers identified:", na2 - na1, "n")
+
cat("Propotion (%) of outliers:", round((na2 - na1) /
sum(!is.na(var_name))*100, 1), "n")
+
cat("Mean of the outliers:", round(mo, 2), "n")
+
m2 <- mean(var_name, na.rm = T)
+
cat("Mean without removing outliers:", round(m1, 2), "n")
+
cat("Mean if we remove outliers:", round(m2, 2), "n")
+
response <- readline(prompt="Do you want to remove outliers and
to replace with NA? [yes/no]: ")
+
if(response == "y" | response == "yes"){
+
dt[as.character(substitute(var))] <- invisible(var_name)
+
assign(as.character(as.list(match.call())$dt), dt, envir =
.GlobalEnv)
+
cat("Outliers successfully removed", "n")
+
 return(invisible(dt))
+
} else{
+
cat("Nothing changed", "n")
+
```

```
            return(invisible(var_name))
        +
        }}
> outlierKD(GlassDataset,RI)

Outliers identified: 17 nPropotion (%) of outliers: 8.6 nMean of the
outliers: 1.52 nMean without removing outliers: 1.52 nMean if we remove
outliers: 1.52 n

Do you want to remove outliers and to replace with NA? [yes/no]: yes

Outliers successfully removed n
```

For now, if we want to check the outliers for relative and absolute humidity, the preceding command is executed and the output generated is shown as follows:

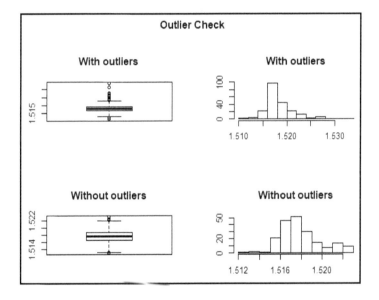

Grubbs' test is basically a test implemented with statistics to identify the outliers in a univariate dataset and even multi-factor datasets assumed to come from a normally distributed population. The following steps are used to evaluate the data frame with core attributes of AH and RH:

1. Install the `outliers` package as shown here, which helps in detecting outliers for the column indicated:

```
> install.packages("outliers")
Installing package into 'C:/Users/Radhika/Documents/R/win-
library/3.5'
          (as 'lib' is unspecified)
          trying URL
'https://cran.rstudio.com/bin/windows/contrib/3.5/outliers_0.14.zip
'
          Content type 'application/zip' length 83897 bytes (81 KB)
          downloaded 81 KB
          package 'outliers' successfully unpacked and MD5 sums
checked
          The downloaded binary packages are in
C:\Users\Radhika\AppData\Local\Temp\Rtmpc1oW5p\downloaded_packages
```

2. Include the necessary libraries to calculate the Grubbs' test as follows:

```
> library(outliers)
Warning message:
          package 'outliers' was built under R version 3.5.2
 > library(ggplot2)
```

3. Create a function for generating flag values of outliers as follows. This function follows the Grubbs' test condition:

```
> grubbs.flag <- function(x) {
+
          outliers <- NULL
   +
          test <- x
   +
          grubbs.result <- grubbs.test(test)
   +
          pv <- grubbs.result$p.value
   +
          while(pv < 0.05) {
   +
              outliers <-
c(outliers,as.numeric(strsplit(grubbs.result$alternative,"
")[[1]][3]))
```

```
+
            test <- x[!x %in% outliers]
+
            grubbs.result <- grubbs.test(test)
+
            pv <- grubbs.result$p.value
+
      }
+
      return(data.frame(X=x,Outlier=(x %in% outliers)))
+
    }
```

4. Call this respective function to analyze the value interpretation of AH and RH as follows:

```
> grubbs.flag(GlassDataset$Na)
X Outlier

1  13.64 FALSE
2  13.89 FALSE
3  13.53 FALSE
4  13.21 FALSE
5  13.27 FALSE
6  12.79 FALSE
7  13.30 FALSE
8  13.15 FALSE
9  14.04 FALSE
10 13.00 FALSE
```

5. If you want a histogram with different colors, you can use the following command:

```
>
ggplot(grubbs.flag(GlassDataset$Na),aes(x=GlassDataset$Na,color=Out
lier,fill=Outlier))+
geom_histogram(binwidth=diff(range(GlassDataset$Na))/0.3)+
theme_bw()
```

This gives us the following output plot:

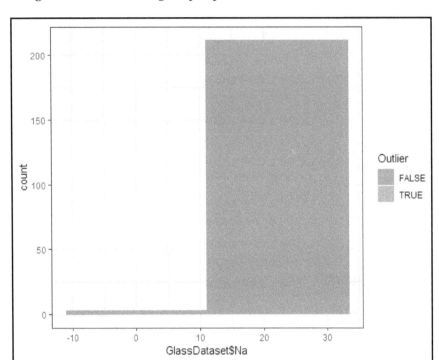

Parsimonious model

Parsimonious models are simple models with great explanatory predictive powers. They usually explain data with a minimum number of parameters, or predictor variables. `MoEClust` is the required R package that fits finite Gaussian Mixtures of Experts models using a range of parsimonious covariance with the help of EM/CEM algorithms.

The following steps need to be carried out to perform parsimonious data analysis:

1. Install the following package, which is needed to create a parsimonious model of our Glass Identification dataset as follows:

    ```
    > install.packages('devtools')
    Installing package into 'C:/Users/Radhika/Documents/R/win-
    library/3.5'
            (as 'lib' is unspecified)
    ```

```
            trying URL
'https://cran.rstudio.com/bin/windows/contrib/3.5/devtools_2.0.2.zi
p'
            Content type 'application/zip' length 383720 bytes (374
KB)
            downloaded 374 KB
            package 'devtools' successfully unpacked and MD5 sums
checked
            The downloaded binary packages are in
C:\Users\Radhika\AppData\Local\Temp\Rtmpc1oW5p\downloaded_packages
            >
            install.packages('MoEClust')
            Installing package into
'C:/Users/Radhika/Documents/R/win-library/3.5'
            (as 'lib' is unspecified)
            trying URL
'https://cran.rstudio.com/bin/windows/contrib/3.5/MoEClust_1.2.1.zi
p'
            Content type 'application/zip' length 759555 bytes (741
KB)
            downloaded 741 KB
            package 'MoEClust' successfully unpacked and MD5 sums
checked
            The downloaded binary packages are in
C:\Users\Radhika\AppData\Local\Temp\Rtmpc1oW5p\downloaded_packages
            >
            library(MoEClust)
            Warning message:
            package 'MoEClust' was built under R version 3.5.3
```

This package helps in clustering the data as per the required value analysis.

2. Create separate data variables with the content parameters in the glass type dataset specified as follows:

```
> View(GlassDataset)
> Glass_Id<-GlassDataset[,1]

> RI<-GlassDataset[,2]

> Mg<-GlassDataset[,4]

> dim(GlassDataset)

[1] 214 11
```

3. For models with covariates in the gating network, or models with equal mixing proportions, there is no need to fit single component models:

```
> m1 <- MoE_clust(Mg, G=0:2, verbose=FALSE)
> m1

Call: MoE_clust(data = Mg, G = 0:2, verbose = FALSE)

Best Model (according to BIC): univariate, equal variance (E), with
2 components

BIC = -509.163 | ICL = -513.038 | AIC = -495.699

No covariates

> m2 <- MoE_clust(Mg, G=2:16, verbose=FALSE)

> m2

Call: MoE_clust(data = Mg, G = 2:16, verbose = FALSE)

Best Model (according to BIC): univariate, equal variance (E), with
5 components

BIC = -341.91 | ICL = -514.979 | AIC = -308.25

No covariates

> m3 <- MoE_clust(Mg, G=16:30, verbose=FALSE)

Warning: For the 24 component models, one or more components were
initialized with only 1 observation

Warning: For the 25 component models, one or more components were
empty after initialization

Warning: For the 26 component models, one or more components were
empty after initialization

Warning: For the 29 component models, one or more components were
empty after initialization

Warning: For the 30 component models, one or more components were
initialized with only 1 observation

> m3

Call: MoE_clust(data = Mg, G = 16:30, verbose = FALSE)
```

```
Best Model (according to BIC): univariate, equal variance (E), with
16 components

BIC = -420.415 | ICL = -897.184 | AIC = -312.704

No covariates

> comp <- MoE_compare(m1, m2)
```

4. This step involves a comparison of the data values and the covariates required, as shown here:

```
> comp <- MoE_compare(m1, m2,m3)
> comp

----------------------------------------------------------------
-----------

Comparison of Gaussian Parsimonious Clustering Models with
Covariates

Data: Mg

----------------------------------------------------------------
-----------

rank MoENames modelNames G df iters bic icl aic loglik gating
expert

1 m2 E 5 10 147 -341.91 -514.979 -308.25 -144.125 None None

2 m2 E 7 14 112 -363.374 -721.646 -316.25 -144.125 None None

3 m2 E 9 18 95 -371.826 -781.495 -311.239 -137.619 None None

equalPro

FALSE

FALSE

FALSE
```

5. Convert the `MoEClust` class to the `Mclust` class in order to visualize the results, with respect to the two options that are required, as shown in the following code:

```
> (mod <- as.Mclust(comp$optimal))
'Mclust' model object: (E,5)

Available components:

[1]  "call" "data" "modelName" "n"

[5]  "d" "G" "BIC" "bic"

[9]  "loglik" "df" "hypvol" "parameters"

[13] "z" "classification" "uncertainty"

> plot(mod, what="classification")

> plot(mod, what="uncertainty")
```

The plot created is as follows:

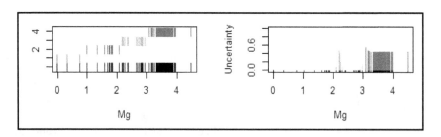

6. The optimal values that are visible in the comparison model can be plotted with the respective values:

```
> plot(comp$optimal, what="gpairs", jitter=FALSE)
```

This gives us the following output plot:

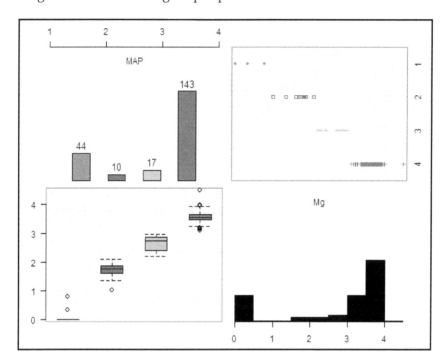

Exploration using graphics

In this section, we will focus on exploring the dataset graphically using a scatter plot, 6-plot, linear correlation plot, linear intercept plot, linear slope plot, and linear residual standard deviation plot.

We will implement the following steps to begin exploration of the data using a graphical structure:

1. This step is intended to depict the scatter plot in two ways. The following scatter plot shows the relationship between the refractive index and the sodium content of glass types:

    ```
    > plot(GlassDataset$Na , GlassDataset$RI, xlab = 'Sodium Content',
    ylab = 'Refractive Index', main = 'Scatter plot for sodium
    content')
    ```

This gives us the following output plot:

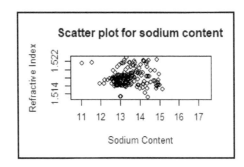

2. The other way to depict the scatter plot is with the help of the `ggplot2` package or library, which is achieved by executing the following command:

```
> library(ggplot2)
> ggplot(data=GlassDataset,aes(x=Id, y=Na)) + geom_point() +
theme_minimal()+geom_col()
```

This gives us the following output plot:

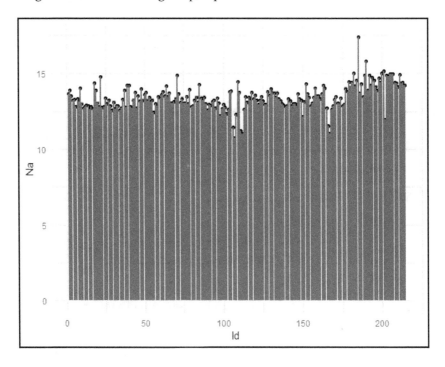

3. Once we remove the columnar representation, we can see that standard scatter plots are created as follows:

```
> ggplot(data=GlassDataset,aes(x=Id, y=Na)) + geom_point() +
theme_minimal()
```

This gives us the following output plot:

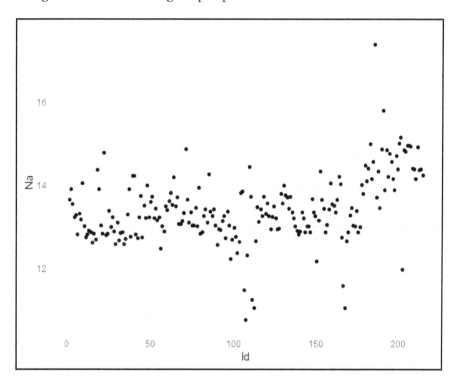

4. Now, we will focus on creating a scatter plot matrix and 3D plots for better visualization and understanding as follows:

```
> library(GGally)
Warning message:

package 'GGally' was built under R version 3.5.2

> ggpairs(GlassDataset)
```

This gives us the following output plot:

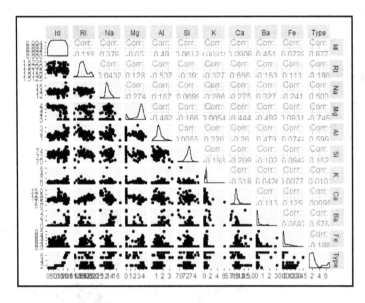

5. The following code block shows the method for creating 3D scatter plots:

```
> library(scatterplot3d)
> scatterplot3d(GlassDataset[,1:3])

Warning message:

Unknown or uninitialised column: 'color'.
```

This gives us the following output plot:

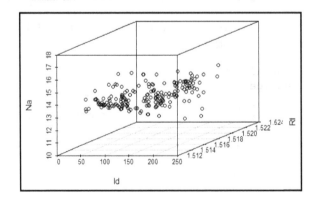

If you are interested in discovering whether there is a relationship between the height of fathers and sons, a correlation coefficient can be calculated to answer this question.

6. This step involves the creation of linear correlation plots. A correlation test is used to evaluate the association between two or more variables.

We'll use the `ggpubr` R package for an easy `ggplot2`-based data visualization, as shown here:

```
> install.packages("ggpubr")
package 'ggrepel' successfully unpacked and MD5 sums checked
package 'ggsci' successfully unpacked and MD5 sums checked
package 'cowplot' successfully unpacked and MD5 sums checked
package 'ggsignif' successfully unpacked and MD5 sums checked
package 'polynom' successfully unpacked and MD5 sums checked
package 'ggpubr' successfully unpacked and MD5 sums checked
The downloaded binary packages are in

C:\Users\Radhika\AppData\Local\Temp\RtmpGirjNl\downloaded_packages

> library(ggpubr)
Loading required package: magrittr
Warning message:
package 'ggpubr' was built under R version 3.5.3
```

7. Let's visualize the data with a scatter plot representation, which is shown as follows:

```
> ggscatter(GlassDataset, x = "RI", y = "Na", add = "reg.line",
conf.int = TRUE, cor.coef = TRUE, cor.method = "pearson", xlab =
"Refractive Index with Sodium Content")
```

This gives us the following output plot:

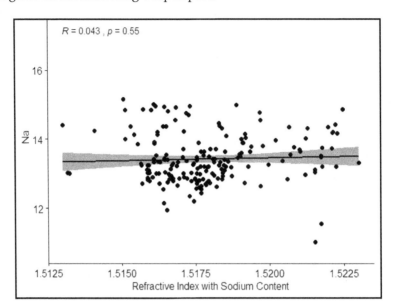

The preliminary test to check the assumptions include the following points:

- Is the covariation linear? Yes, from the preceding plot, the relationship is linear. In the situation where the scatter plots show curved patterns, we are dealing with a nonlinear association between the two variables.
- Does the data from each of the two variables *(x, y)* follow a normal distribution? Use the Shapiro-Wilk normality test, which has `shapiro.test()` as the R function, and look at the normality plot that has `ggpubr::ggqqplot()` as the R function.

The Shapiro-Wilk test is a hypothesis test that can be used to perform the following activities for the dataset indicated. The crucial activities regarding different types of hypothesis are as follows:

- **Null hypothesis**: The data is normally distributed
- **Alternative hypothesis**: The data is not normally distributed

The following steps are used to perform the Shapiro-Wilk test for our dataset:

```
> shapiro.test(GlassDataset$RI)
Shapiro-Wilk normality test

data: GlassDataset$RI
W = 0.94365, p-value = 5.733e-07

> shapiro.test(GlassDataset$Na)
Shapiro-Wilk normality test
data: GlassDataset$Na
W = 0.94576, p-value = 3.466e-07
```

We will now carry out the visual inspection of the data normality using Q-Q plots (quantile-quantile plots). Q-Q plots draw the correlation between a given sample and the normal distribution, as shown here:

```
> ggqqplot(GlassDataset$RI, ylab = "RI")
> ggqqplot(GlassDataset$Na, ylab = "Na")
```

This gives us the following output plot for `RI`:

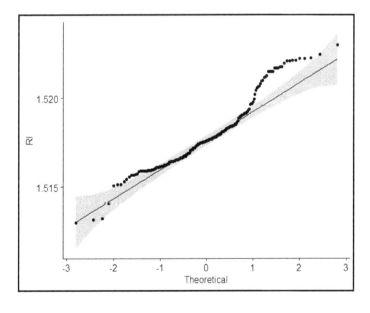

This gives us the following output plot for `Na`:

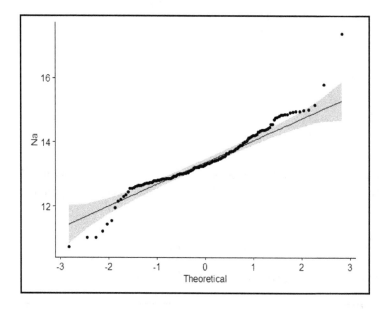

From the normality plots, we conclude that both populations may come from normal distributions.

Now, let's perform the Pearson correlation test between two variables to analyze optimization and regression problems in further detail as follows:

```
> res <- cor.test(GlassDataset$RI, GlassDataset$Na,
+
                        method = "pearson")
> res

            Pearson's product-moment correlation
    data: GlassDataset$RI and GlassDataset$Na
    t = 0.60403, df = 195, p-value = 0.5465
    alternative hypothesis: true correlation is not equal to 0
    95 percent confidence interval:
     -0.09716752 0.18191195
    sample estimates:
        cor
    0.04321522
```

If we plot the correlation values generated, especially the `p.value` compared with parameters, we get the following graphical representation:

```
> plot(res$p.value, res$parameter)
> res$p.value
[1] 0.5465245
```

We then get the following plot:

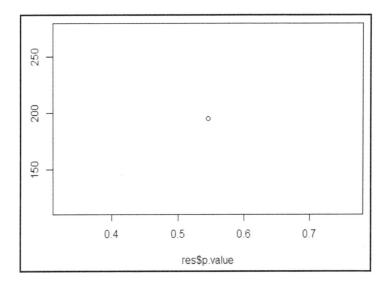

As the p-value of the test is less than the significance level, alpha = 0.05, we can conclude that `RI` and `Na` are significantly correlated with correlation coefficients.

The `cor.test()` function returns a list containing the following components:

- `p.value`: The p-value of the test
- `estimate`: The correlation coefficient

```
> res$p.value
[1] 0.5465245
>   res$estimate
cor
0.04321522
```

The **Kendall rank correlation coefficient**, or **Kendall's Tau**, statistic is used to estimate a rank-based measure of association. This test may be used if the data does not necessarily come from a bivariate normal distribution:

```
>   res2 <- cor.test(GlassDataset$RI, GlassDataset$Na,  method="kendall")
>   res2
                    Kendall's rank correlation tau
        data: GlassDataset$RI and GlassDataset$Na
        z = 1.4702, p-value = 0.1415
        alternative hypothesis: true tau is not equal to 0
        sample estimates:
              tau
        0.07070823
```

The conclusions generated are as follows:

- The correlation coefficient is between -1 and 1.
- A figure of -1 indicates a strong negative correlation. This means that every time x increases, y decreases.
- A result of 0 means that there is no association between the two variables (x and y).
- A figure of 1 indicates a strong positive correlation. This means that y increases with x.

Summary

In this chapter, we have focused on the implementation of all libraries for handling optimization as well as regression data problems from the data frame indicated. The best illustration that is considered is to check the various parameters of the Glass Identification dataset where it includes various parameters of minerals for assessment, such as Na, Mg, and many more. We have listed some of the various packages that are available for reading in various kinds of attributes within the dataset mentioned in R. In the later sections, we covered the various correlation aspects that help to maintain linear regression analysis for the data frame indicated.

In the next chapter, we will cover how to build a roadmap for you to build on the skills you learned in this book. We will also cover how to gain further expertise in the field of data science with R.

4
Section 4: Conclusions

Now that you have finished the book, you might be wondering how to get help when you get stuck, or you might be thinking about what to learn next to enhance your data science career.

These issues are addressed in the following chapter:

Chapter 11, *Next Steps*

11
Next Steps

This chapter will help you to build a roadmap for yourself, for building upon the skills you have learned in this book, and with which you can gain further expertise in the field of data science with R. It will list what other skills you can learn next, how you can build a data science portfolio, and how to find publicly available datasets to use in your projects. Also, it will give guidance on how to get help when you are stuck on a data exploration issue.

The following topics will be covered in this chapter:

- What to learn next
- Building a data science portfolio
- Finding publicly available datasets to use in your projects
- Getting help when you get stuck with a data exploration problem

Technical requirements

You should have hands-on experience or knowledge of the following points before getting started with this chapter:

- R programming language
- RStudio
- R packages
  (including `readr`, `readxl`, `jsonlite`, `httr`, `rvest`, `DBI`, `dplyr`, `stringr`, `forcats`, `lubridate`, `hms`, `blob`, `ggplot2`, and `knitr`)

What to learn next

In the previous chapters, we experienced a variety of implementations with various datasets with the main focus on performing various statistical approaches with the R tool. The R programming language can be tricky for data scientists with limited programming experience. Therefore, it is considered important to create a learning path for R.

Creating this learning path for R was a continuous trade-off between being pragmatic and exhaustive. Therefore, we decided on creating the outline for the learning path.

The outline for the learning path is as follows:

- Why R?
- Environmental setup.
- Gist to R syntax and its pattern.
- Primary packages.
- Understanding the `help` system in R.
- The data analysis workflow:
    - Data import
    - Manipulating data
    - Visualizing data
    - Presenting the results
    - Standout as R wizard

Why R?

R is always considered an important language for data science implementation. The functions and libraries in R include content contributed by academics and statistician. It is widely regarded to be as good as SAS, STATA, and SPSS. As per the survey conducted in IEEE in the year 2015, R has gained popularity among the top ten languages.

R is known for its diversity with task implementation in domains such as finance, statistics, and real estate. The user implementing R will definitely be able to see a diverse set of examples and applications on a daily basis, which helps in achieving accurate solutions.

Environmental setup

R is an open source software, and all you need to do is download a copy in your local system and install it as needed. It includes the best supporting IDE called RStudio, which we have implemented throughout this book. There is one more IDE, namely Architect, which can be used on a trial and error basis for users to experiment with something new.

R is pretty straightforward when it comes to its installation procedure and there are binaries available for all operating systems from the **Comprehensive R Archive Network (CRAN)**, at `https://cran.r-project.org/`. This feature is quite unique, as R does not limit itself to one operating system.

The useful links are as follows:

- `https://cran.r-project.org/mirrors.html`
- `https://www.rstudio.com/products/rstudio/download/`

R syntax

Understanding the syntax of R includes the same pattern of learning a computer language, as the base and the platform to be used are quite different and it involves a lot of practice.

There are various key points that you should understand, such as the variable declaration in R. It is as easy as the following example:

```
> x<- c(1,2,3)
> x
[1] 1 2 3
```

Viewing a particular dataset includes the implementation of only one function, as follows:

```
> View(cars)
```

R packages

R packages include a bundle of code that is designed for a specific purpose, and can be reused by a group of developers. Packages include information of data, documentation, and tests. It is very simple to download a particular package and start using its features.

The following set of commands are used for installation and inclusion of the package in the required workspace:

```
> install.packages("ggplot2")
> library(ggplot2)
```

Alternatively, the following can be used:

```
> require(ggplot2)
```

Understanding the help system

The R programming language includes a built-in help system. The best demonstration is the implementation of the following command:

```
> plot
```

The preceding command execution will provide the user with the complete documentation on the `plot` function.

The complete documentation will be visible, as follows:

plot {graphics}   R Documentation

Generic X-Y Plotting

Description

Generic function for plotting of R objects. For more details about the graphical parameter arguments, see par.

For simple scatter plots, plot.default will be used. However, there are plot methods for many R objects, including functions, data.frames, density objects, etc. Use methods(plot) and the documentation for these.

Usage

plot(x, y, ...)

Arguments

x   the coordinates of points in the plot. Alternatively, a single plotting structure, function or *any R object with a* plot *method* can be provided

y   the y coordinates of points in the plot, *optional* if x is an appropriate structure.

R places a strong importance on its documentation. R documentation (`https://www.rdocumentation.org/`) includes different documentation for many packages and functions.

Stack Overflow (`https://stackoverflow.com/questions/tagged/r`) is another resource for getting answers to questions on common implementation of R questions with suitable solutions.

The data analysis workflow

The main sections of the data analysis workflow are outlined in the following subheadings.

Data import

Before getting started with data analysis, it is important that you have knowledge about the data. The best part is that you can import datasets in R in any format, such as Excel, CSV, or text files. The toughest part is that importing the dataset of a different type necessitates a different approach.

Manipulating data

Manipulating data with R is considered a vast topic, as it includes various sections and packages with proper implementation. There are a number of packages in R that a user should grasp when data manipulations are performed.

Visualizing data

The core reason why R is considered a favorite tool of data analysts and scientists is because of its visualization capabilities. We had a look at the necessary libraries that are needed for data visualization in `Chapter 1`, *Setting Up Our Data Analysis Environment*. Now, it is important to keep practicing them effectively.

Reporting results

The best approach to present the data models or data visualizations is through dynamic documents or reports, such as PDF documents. R Markdown (`https://rmarkdown.rstudio.com/`) is considered a perfect tool for creating data reports in a reproducible manner in specific formats, such as HTML, Word, or PDF.

Standout as R wizard

R is considered an evolving and progressing language. It includes features for academics and businesses, which are huge and skyrocketing, with the inclusion of new features that are considered to be very resourceful. More practice with various datasets will help us improve our knowledge of this programming language.

Building a data science portfolio

Now as you get accustomed to a particular language, whether it is R or Python, it is mandatory that you create your own portfolio. Kindly refer to the following steps, which include an approach to creating your own data science portfolio:

- **Be visible**: Always keep your profile updated with your required skillsets to keep yourself visible in the market.
- **Articulate your ability**: Try out different features and experiments, and check on the output you get. This will help to articulate your ability and skills for any area of data science.
- **Be visual**: Always have a look at the trending technologies and the programming languages that are being used. Keep up to date with the algorithms, as algorithms form the base of any implementation.
- **Showcase process**: Include your own algorithms and experiments. Try to showcase them as and when needed.
- **Stand out from the crowd**: Always maintain a level of confidence that will help you to stand out uniquely from the crowd of data scientists or engineers.

Datasets in R

It is mandatory to have knowledge about freely-available datasets in R, which are built in and can be used as and when needed.

To have a look at the built-in datasets, all you need to do is execute the following command and call the required dataset:

```
> library(datasets)
```

You can call the required dataset and have a look at its description. Rstudio is considered to have the best feature for showing descriptions of datasets, as follows:

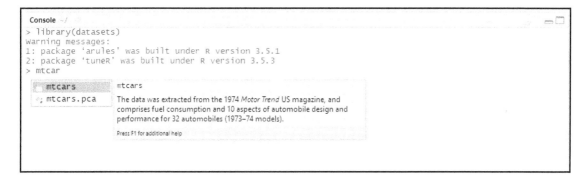

The popular datasets that are available in R are mentioned as follows, with descriptions and dimensions:

Dataset	Description	Rows	Columns
airquality	This includes New York air quality measurements.	153	6
anscombe	This consists of Anscombe's quartet of *identical* simple linear regressions.	11	8
attenu	This dataset is all about the Joyner-Boore attenuation data.	182	5
attitude	This dataset includes the Chatterjee-Price attitude data.	30	7
chickwts	This dataset includes chicken weights by feed type.	71	2
EuStockMarkets	This is considered as a popular dataset that includes daily closing prices of major European stock indices for 1991–1998.	1860	4
faithful	This consists of Old Faithful Geyser data.	272	2
Formaldehyde	This consists of information about formaldehyde.	6	2

Loblolly	This consists growth details of Loblolly pine trees.	84	3
longley	This consists numeric values like GNP for Longley's economic regression data.	16	7
lynx	This includes all details of annual Canadian Lynx trappings for 1821–1934.	114	2
morley	This consists of Michelson speed of light data.	100	3
mtcars	This is the most popular dataset that includes details of motor trend car road tests.	32	11

Getting help with exploratory data analysis

Exploratory data analysis (EDA) in R or any other programming language is nothing but one aspect of a research project or any data-based investigation. Basically, it involves everything, such as manipulation, cleaning, wrangling, and data visualization.
EDA involves all of the algorithms for data analysis, which is similar to the data manipulation process. Always refer to online solutions and documentation of R (https://www.rdocumentation.org/) for getting the appropriate help when you get stuck with a data exploration problem.

Summary

In this chapter, we have listed a complete approach to understanding the R language. The roadmap of learning R provides an approach to help you master this language. Success and ease of use with data analysis implementation and inferences come with more practice. It is considered the best solution to experiment with various algorithms and the built-in datasets of R in order to become an expert in exploratory data analysis.

Other Books You May Enjoy

If you enjoyed this book, you may be interested in these other books by Packt:

R Deep Learning Projects
Yuxi (Hayden) Liu, Pablo Maldonado

ISBN: 978-1-78847-840-3

- Instrument Deep Learning models with packages such as deepnet, MXNetR, Tensorflow, H2O, Keras, and text2vec
- Apply neural networks to perform handwritten digit recognition using MXNet
- Get the knack of CNN models, Neural Network API, Keras, and TensorFlow for traffic sign classification
- Implement credit card fraud detection with Autoencoders
- Master reconstructing images using variational autoencoders
- Wade through sentiment analysis from movie reviews
- Run from past to future and vice versa with bidirectional Long Short-Term Memory (LSTM) networks
- Understand the applications of Autoencoder Neural Networks in clustering and dimensionality reduction

Machine Learning with R

Brett Lantz

ISBN: 978-1-78829-586-4

- Discover the origins of machine learning and how exactly a computer learns by example
- Prepare your data for machine learning work with the R programming language
- Classify important outcomes using nearest neighbor and Bayesian methods
- Predict future events using decision trees, rules, and support vector machines
- Forecast numeric data and estimate financial values using regression methods
- Model complex processes with artificial neural networks — the basis of deep learning
- Avoid bias in machine learning models
- Evaluate your models and improve their performance
- Connect R to SQL databases and emerging big data technologies such as Spark, H2O, and TensorFlow

Leave a review - let other readers know what you think

Please share your thoughts on this book with others by leaving a review on the site that you bought it from. If you purchased the book from Amazon, please leave us an honest review on this book's Amazon page. This is vital so that other potential readers can see and use your unbiased opinion to make purchasing decisions, we can understand what our customers think about our products, and our authors can see your feedback on the title that they have worked with Packt to create. It will only take a few minutes of your time, but is valuable to other potential customers, our authors, and Packt. Thank you!

Index

R

R command prompt
  R packages, installing from 14
R documentation
  reference 241
R Markdown
  about 76
  installing 76, 77
  reference 242
  working with 78
R packages
  about 239
  installing 13
  installing, from R command prompt 14
  installing, from RStudio 14, 15
R syntax 239
R tools
  installing 13
R
  datasets 243, 244
  environmental setup 239
  Help command 240
  need for 238
  reference 58
read_delim method 22, 23
read_fwf method 23
read_log method 24
read_table method 23
read_tsv method 21, 22
readr R package
  rectangular data, converting into R 18, 20
readr read functions
  about 21
  read_delim method 22, 23
  read_fwf method 23
  read_log method 24
  read_table method 23
  read_tsv method 21, 22
readxl R package
  data, reading from Excel files 25, 26
rectangular data
  converting, into R 18, 20
reproducible data analysis reports
  customizing 84, 86

exporting 84, 86
  with knitr 79, 81, 83
residual plots 72, 73
RStudio
  installation link 9
  installation links 239
  R packages, installing from 14, 15
rvest package
  data, obtaining into R 29

S

scatter plots 59, 61, 62
selecting and filtering, data
  about 49
  filter() function 50
  functions 49
  select() function 49
Shapiro-Wilk test 116, 117
simplification process 27
spectrum plots
  creating 144
Stack Overflow
  reference 241
statistical hypothesis 102
statistical hypothesis, types
  about 102
  alternative hypothesis 102
  null hypothesis 102
Structured Query Language (SQL) 45

T

Tietjen-Moore test 105, 107
time series datasets, data visualization
  about 140
  autocorrelation plot, creating 140, 143
  phase plots, creating 145, 146
  spectrum plots, creating 144
time series datasets, Hypothesis test
  about 128
  directional hypothesis 129
  t-test 129
time series datasets
  about 119, 120, 122
  Bartlett's test 138, 139
  data structure 126, 128

www.ingramcontent.com/pod-product-compliance
Lightning Source LLC
Chambersburg PA
CBHW080634060326
40690CB00021B/4926